REMARKS

ON THE

MYSORE BLUE-BOOK,

WITH A FEW WORDS TO

MR. R. D. MANGLES

REMARKS

ON THE

MYSORE BLUE-BOOK,

WITH A FEW WORDS TO

MR. R. D. MANGLES

BY

MAJOR EVANS BELL

GYAN

Published by

Gyan Publishing House
5, Ansari Road
Daryaganj, New Delhi-110002
Phone: 011-47034999, 9811692060
E-mail: books@gyanbooks.com

Distribution Network
gyanbooks.com
India, USA, Canada, UK, Australia

ISBN: 978-93-6433-135-7 (PB)
First Published, 1866

2nd Impression 2024

Printed at: Gyan Press, Delhi.

REMARKS ON THE MYSORE BLUE-BOOK
Author: MAJOR EVANS BELL

REMARKS

ON THE

MYSORE BLUE-BOOK,

WITH A FEW WORDS TO

MR. R. D. MANGLES:

BY

MAJOR EVANS BELL,

LATE OF THE MADRAS STAFF CORPS,

AUTHOR OF "THE MYSORE REVERSION," "THE EMPIRE IN INDIA," "THE ENGLISH IN INDIA," ETC.

"Machiavel's errors arose not in consulting the principle of utility, but in making false applications of it. Bad faith is always bad policy."

JEREMY BENTHAM.

LONDON:

TRÜBNER AND CO., PATERNOSTER ROW.

1866.

"I consider that, in fact, our Government is at the head of a system composed of native States, and I would avoid what are called rightful occasions of appropriating those territories. On the contrary, I should be disposed, as far as I could, to maintain the native States, and I am satisfied that their maintenance, and the giving to the subjects of those States the conviction that they are considered permanent parts of the general Government of India, would naturally strengthen our authority."

LORD ELLENBOROUGH, 1853.

"The house may dismiss at once all question of the annexation of territory. There are many reasons why I think we should not annex Native States. It is for our advantages that such States should be left in India."

SIR CHARLES WOOD, now LORD HALIFAX, in the House of Commons, 26th Feb., 1863.

"Thirty years ago the predominant idea with many English statesmen was that our interest in India consisted in extending our territory to the largest possible extent. To that annexation policy the terrible disaster of the mutiny of 1857 must to a large extent be ascribed. But as time has gone on, that desire of increased dominion which is the natural temptation of all powerful States has been overcome, and Statesmen of all parties have arrived at the conclusion that we now hold in India pretty well as much as we can govern, and that we should be pursuing an unwise and dangerous policy if we tried to extend our borders or to lessen the power or the permanence of those native rulers upon whose assistance we have so long relied. I believe the native Princes were formerly the objects of jealousy and distrust to English rulers, but within the last ten years a great change has come over the spirit of our statesmanship in that respect; and there is now, I think, a general desire to uphold them in the rights and honours which they justly earned by their loyal support at the time of the mutiny, and to look upon them not as impediments to our rule, but as its most useful auxiliaries."

LORD CRANBORNE at Stamford, July 12, 1866.

PREFACE.

I HAVE endeavoured to make more clear in the latter part of these pages what I have already urged in previous publications, that acquiescence in continued annexation means really the refusal of permanent reform.

Since the first edition of the *Mysore Reversion* was published in January 1865, two events, calculated to affect materially the ultimate settlement in this matter, have occurred,—the Rajah's formal and public adoption of a son on the 18th June, 1865; and the appearance of the Papers Relating to Mysore, moved for by Sir Henry Rawlinson in the House of Commons, on the 27th February, 1866.

It may be gathered, as well from the contents of the Blue-Book as from general conversation, that there are four current objections to the restoration of a Native Government in Mysore. (1) The reversionary right of the Paramount Power to take that country by "lapse"; (2) the duty of the Paramount Power to secure a good administration for the people; (3) the great weight and authority of those who recommend the annexation; and (4) the necessity of our Government maintaining at all hazards the consistency and inflexibility of its own well-considered decisions. In the following pages I have attempted to dispose of the two first objections as they present themselves in the official despatches. A few words must be said here as to the two last.

The argument of authority amounts to little more than

this,—that five successive occupants of the Viceregal Chair, Lords Dalhousie, Canning and Elgin, Sir William Denison and Sir John Lawrence, have all returned adverse replies to the Rajah's repeated applications; and that a majority of the Council of India, the constitutional advisers of Her Majesty's Secretary of State, have also decided against his Highness's claims. This formidable array is, however, much weaker than it appears at the first glance.

No one can have any doubt that Lord Dalhousie would have annexed Mysore on the demise of the reigning Rajah. But he would have done so by the same process that was used to dispose of the Sattara, Nagpore, and Jhansi States, and the mediatised Principality of the Carnatic; and as his constant supporter, Mr. Mangles, has done in this instance, he would have adduced the worst of these cases as satisfactory precedents. So that if we accept Lord Dalhousie as an authority, we must approve in general the principles, the procedure and the results of his territorial acquisitions. And I trust that no British statesman, except perhaps the Duke of Argyll, is at the present day prepared to go quite as far as that.

Lord Canning was not really hostile to the Rajah's right of adopting a successor. He admitted it in principle, and withdrew from those false positions under which for some years the unjust prerogative of nullifying adoptions had been practised. He unquestionably looked upon Mysore as a very desirable acquisition; but he had been misled into the belief that the Rajah did not wish to adopt a son, and would bequeath his dominions to the British Government. Lord Canning cannot be quoted as an authority adverse to the Rajah's rights.

Lord Elgin's lamented death after so brief a tenure of office has left in doubt the course he would have taken. It is understood that he was desirous of negotiating a settlement of the Rajah's claim of restoration by a sort of compromise. Lord Elgin's authority, therefore, is by no means injurious to the Rajah's cause.

Sir William Denison was called unexpectedly to take provisional charge of the Viceregal office, and the letter of the 31st December, 1863, communicating the refusal of the Home Government to replace the Rajah at the head of his own administration, was obviously signed by him as a simple matter of routine. He could not have avoided explaining the Secretary of State's decision. The more important question of maintaining or destroying the State of Mysore arose at a later date, and did not demand the consideration either of Lord Elgin or of Sir William Denison.

Whatever may have been the views expressed by Sir John Lawrence since he returned to the latitude of Calcutta, he is understood to have been favourably disposed towards the Rajah, when he was a Member of the Council in the more pure and free atmosphere of London. I think I have succeeded in proving in the succeeding pages that his altered opinions are not the result of a more careful scrutiny of the facts, or of a deeper consideration of causes and consequences.

The mass of Viceregal authority is thus reduced after our our analysis to that of Lord Dalhousie and his most distinguished Lieutenant; and the annexation of Mysore is seen to be a mere return to that policy which has shaken throughout Asia the belief in British honour, and which has been denounced, more or less plainly, by every leading statesman of Great Britain.

But let us turn to the other side, and read the list of those who are known to have supported, and who now recommend, the policy of good faith, restitution and solid reform. Lord William Bentinck, who, under the influence of exaggerated reports, assumed the management of Mysore, regretted the hasty step he had taken, and proposed the

Rajah's restoration to the head of a more limited Government. His two immediate successors, Lord Metcalfe and Lord Auckland, concurred in the advisability of restoring the Rajah to power, and the former characterised the suspension of his Highness as "a harsh and unprovoked measure." Sir William Hay Macnaghten, who was Foreign Secretary at Calcutta, when that Report of 1833 was submitted which first revealed to Lord William Bentinck the truth about Mysore, has left in writing his opinion that the Rajah had been "visited with undue severity," and his wish that "a portion of his country should be restored to him." Lord Hardinge recorded his doubts of the legality of the Rajah's supersession.

Lord Glenelg, who had been President of the Board of Control when the Government of Mysore was taken out of the Rajah's hands, was always of opinion that our action ought to have been curative, not destructive of the dependent State; and to the last day of his long life the venerable statesman was anxious to hear of the Rajah's full restoration.

The late Mr. Casamajor, who was Resident at Mysore when the Rajah was superseded, and General Briggs, who was the first Commissioner for the government of Mysore after the supersession, have both declared that the total exclusion of the Rajah from public life was unnecessarily severe, and has been unwarrantably prolonged. General Briggs, who after a long and distinguished career in India, has won a reputation in Europe by his labours in Oriental literature, history and statistics, has signed a petition to the House of Commons, (presented on the 10th August, 1866,) praying that Mysore may not be annexed, but that a native government may be reestablished, "with every possible security for British interests, and for the prosperity and happiness of the people of the country."

That petition was also signed by General Sir John Low,

late Member of the Supreme Council of India; by General J. S. Fraser, for fifteen years Resident at Hyderabad, and previously Resident at Travancore and at Mysore; by Colonel Haines, late Judicial Commissioner of Mysore; by Major-General White of the Madras Army, who was Assistant to the Resident of Mysore when the Rajah's personal government was suspended; by Sir Robert Hamilton, late Governor-General's Agent in Central India; by General Le Grand Jacob, whose influence and popularity with the Chiefs and leading men, and his abilities both as a soldier and a civil ruler, alone prevented the flame of rebellion from spreading in 1857-8 over Kolapore and the Southern Mahratta Country; by Mr. W. H. Bayley, late Secretary to the Madras Government; by Colonel French, late Resident at Jodhpore and at Baroda; by Mr. T. L. Blane, late a Member of the Madras Board of Revenue; by Colonel G. Williams, formerly Commissioner of Military Police, and who was by Lord Canning's side throughout those critical months of the insurrection, when the government of the North West Provinces was conducted at Allahabad by the Viceroy himself; by Captain Felix Jones, late Resident in the Persian Gulf; by Captain Frushard, late of the Indian Navy, and by about fifty other gentlemen, many of them having served in the Civil and Military Services of India, and many being well-known as authors and men of science.

Only two of the majority in the Council of India, Mr. Mangles and Mr. Prinsep, have attempted to put into writing some answer to the powerful arguments of their five colleagues, Sir George Clerk, Sir Henry Montgomery, Sir John Willoughby, Captain Eastwick, and Sir Frederick Currie. My readers must judge how I have dealt with the Minutes of these two Councillors, who, as I have shown, are so deeply committed by their antecedent acts and pledges, that a strong bias against the Rajah's claims could hardly fail to be entertained by both of them.

It can scarcely be said, after due consideration of these facts, that the balance of authority inclines against the opinion held by the minority of the Council of India.

There remains to be considered what may be called the argument of *prestige*. It has been urged that the reversal of a decision, deliberately and repeatedly promulgated by the Viceroy of India in Council, and approved by the Secretary of State, would ruin the *prestige* of Government, and—to make use of words attributed to an official of rank at Calcutta—would shake the very foundations of British power.

This argument appears to me not only to be devoid of all moral principle, but to be directly opposed to sound political science. The *prestige* of an Imperial Government—that awe and respect by which order and obedience are preserved among its subjects and its dependent Allies,—is based partly on a belief in its material resources, partly on faith in its moral superiority. The obstinate maintenance of an unjust decree, after its injustice has been publicly exposed, cannot augment material strength, and must destroy moral influence. Such persistent wrong does not even tend to strike terror; it rather inspires disdain.

No doubt when the professional rulers of Calcutta have written "able" and "elaborate" Minutes, despatches, demi-official and private letters innumerable, in defence of a decision embodying all their traditional and characteristic prejudices, until they have set their hearts on the issue, the reversal of that decision must be extremely mortifying to them, and must diminish their personal *prestige* very much with the outer world. And I can fully understand and admit that anything which lowers the credit and dignity of the higher officials, especially of the Viceregal Government, in the eyes of the people of India, is so far disadvantageous and regrettable. But the counterbalancing disadvantages of refusing redress, would be very much greater in many cases, and eminently in this particular case. Such a refusal would not only lower the credit of the Government of India more than could possibly be done by the reversal of their decision, but would carry discredit into more remote and vital regions of the State: it would dishonour Her Majesty's Government; it would sully the Crown. Loss of respect for the Crown would be much more hurtful to the Empire than loss of respect for any individual Minister or Lieutenant, however exalted in rank or station. The officials of the day, their exploits and their failures, their glories and their mortifications, come and go, and pass away; but the Imperial Government remains; and if it accepts and confirms a wrong, can never shift the responsibility, or shake off the stigma. The loss of credit to a Judge, when his decree is reversed on appeal, is very trifling; but the general administration of justice would fall into complete disrepute if appeals were never heard, and every decree were irreversible. In political affairs, where there is no code of substantive law, an unlimited right of appeal is absolutely essential; and if the appellate jurisdiction is seen in important matters to be no idle form, no real discredit need fall on the "Court below." And even if the Provincial Government be so deeply committed by its previous pertinacity that it cannot accept a defeat without some little show of discomfiture, the love and honour gained for the general system of Imperial Government, would far outweigh the temporary disparagement, if any there be, that is thrown on local authority.

When, for instance, the little Principality of Dhar was at last restored to the administration of its native Ruler, in consequence of the public-spirited efforts of the most vigilant and energetic of Indian Reformers, Mr. John Dickinson, no doubt the effect was by no means pleasant to the feelings of Sir John Lawrence and Colonel Durand, —more especially of the latter, who, in his successive capacities, as Political Agent in Central India, as Member of the Council in London, and as Foreign Secretary at Calcutta, had endeavoured first to secure the annexation of Dhar, then its management for an indefinite period by a British officer, and lastly the imposition upon the Rajah of a Minister who was personally disagreeable to him.* When the Government of India was driven from these positions one after the other, and directed to carry out an effectual restoration, in consequence of Mr. Dickinson's persevering exposure, and the firmness of Lord Stanley, then in opposition, who as Secretary of State had originally saved the Rajah from the dethronement recommended by Colonel Durand, that officer in particular, and several members of the Government of India, may naturally have felt as if a slight had been cast upon their judgment and discretion, and may have feared that their personal weight and credit would be lowered in the eyes of the public. And to a certain extent this fear may have been well-founded. But most certainly the prestige and popularity of the Imperial Government were not lowered but raised, nor was the cheerful allegiance of the Princes and Chieftains of Central India weakened, but on the contrary strengthened, by the restoration of Dhar, after a period of beneficial and frugal management, the credit of which is almost entirely due, as I willingly admit, to the judicious instructions of the Calcutta Foreign Office. The successful examples of Dhar, Kolapore, and Travancore, restored to their native Princes after effectual reformation, will form better precedents for the settlement of Mysore than the disastrous cases of Sattara and Jhansi.

* *Dhar not Restored*, and *A Sequel to Dhar not Restored*, by John Dickinson, F.R.A.S., (King, Parliament Street,) 1864 and 1865; and the Parliamentary Papers, *Further Correspondence Relating to Dhar*, 1865.

The generous concessions of the Sovereign, in a time of peace and prosperity, do not produce an impression of weakness, but of strength and confidence. And a great work of restitution may easily be conducted as a royal act of grace and favour, so as to convey no ostensible censure or reproof to those who have hitherto opposed it.

The real political danger in India is not what it has been recently represented. The danger is not that the Viceroy's authority will be despised, but the Queen's. There is no danger that the tributary and protected Princes and their Ministers and adherents will learn to look for orders to London instead of Calcutta in ordinary matters. The danger is that if in their extraordinary emergencies an appeal to Great Britain is found to be nugatory, they may say in their despair, "There is no Imperial Power; there is no Parliament; there is no Sovereign over us; there is only a Collector."

REMARKS

ON THE

MYSORE BLUE-BOOK.

THE PAPERS "relative to the claims of the Rajah of Mysore to be restored to the government of his territories, and to be allowed to adopt an heir," called for by Sir Henry Rawlinson, and ordered by the House of Commons to be printed on the 13th March, 1866, authenticate the more important documents published in the first edition of the *Mysore Reversion*, and will, I think, fully prove that I have neither overstated the case in favour of the Rajah, nor understated the adverse case set up against him. Not one of the despatches from the Governor-General in Council, or from the Secretary of State, which now see the light for the first time, nor even the hostile Minutes by Mr. Ross Donnelly Mangles and Mr. H. Thoby Prinsep, contain a single fact or allegation against the Rajah's character or conduct which I have not already noticed; and not a single argument, whether based on right or policy, is advanced against his cause which I may not claim to have met and refuted.

On the other hand, the Papers include Minutes of Dissent from the instructions sent to India in this matter, recorded by five of the most distinguished Members of the Council of India—Sir George Clerk, Sir Frederick Currie, Sir John Willoughby, Sir Henry Montgomery, and Captain W. J. Eastwick,—all of whom support the Rajah's claims, in general accordance with the views contained in my book.

The objections, urged with earnestness almost amounting to vehemence, by so many men of grave character and large experience, might well give pause to the most remorseless advocate of annexation. Even Lord Dalhousie, in his Minute of the 30th August, 1848, printed in the *Sattara Papers* of 1849 (p. 83), when recommending that no just opportunity of taking possession of Native States by the process of "lapse," should be omitted, declared that "wherever a shadow of doubt can be shown, the claim should at once be abandoned." The solemn protests recorded by the minority of the Secretary of State's Council—a minority so strong in acknowledged ability and high reputation,—ought surely to be sufficient to raise more than that "shadow of a doubt" which Lord Dalhousie held should lead to the abandonment of such a design.

If the Rajah's case is so far plausible, and the adverse claim so far questionable, as to admit of the gravest scruples being entertained by five eminently competent judges, all of whose instincts and prejudices would naturally lead them to coincide with the majority, we ought seriously to reflect on the impression that must be produced in India on those who naturally sympathise with the Rajah, and who cannot help feeling that the downfall of the State may form a precedent for the ruin of their own dearest interests and for the destruction of all they hold sacred.

When Sir Henry Montgomery is seen to accuse his own Government of "*a breach of good faith;*" when Sir John Willoughby denounces "*the flagrant injustice*" of the decision; when Sir Frederick Currie declares it to be "*unjust and illegal, and a violation of special treaties, which the British Government have bound themselves to maintain inviolate;*" when Sir George Clerk condemns it as "*the result of wild counsel prompting the indiscriminate gratification of a selfish policy,*" "*unworthy of a great nation,*" neither "*honest nor dignified,*" and regrets that so "*loyal a Prince*" should be made "*the victim of such extreme measures;*" and when Captain Eastwick asserts that the treatment of the Rajah "*cannot be justified by our treaty obligations, nor by the law and practice of*

India;" what can we expect to be said and thought on the subject by the dependent Sovereigns of India and their advisers and adherents?

This Blue-Book may do infinite good or infinite harm. If the publication does not save the Principality of Mysore, it will, by displaying the origin, progress, and pretexts of the scheme for its extinction, and the cogent reasoning by which these pretexts were refuted, aggravate and extend the worst effects of this mischievous and short-sighted measure, and remove every shadow of excuse or palliation.

The most remarkable feature of the arguments adduced in the Despatches and Minutes adverse to the Rajah's claims, is that they are invariably based upon the most obvious contradictions and misstatements of facts officially recorded. For instance, in the despatch from the Governor-General in Council to the Secretary of State, dated 31st August, 1864, it is said that "by twenty years of misrule, by extravagance, venality, and oppression, resulting in the rebellion of his subjects, who, but for the interference of the British Government, would have shaken off his authority, the Maharajah violated the conditions which were the basis of his dominion, and forced the British Government to the exercise of the sovereign power, which, under the 4th Article of the Subsidiary Treaty, they had retained, of superseding the Maharajah's rule, and of carrying on the government of Mysore in their own name and by their sole authority."*

The terms in which the misgovernment and its results are denounced, are exaggerated far beyond what the facts warrant; but it is simply untrue that the 4th Article of the Subsidiary Treaty gives the Honourable Company the power of "superseding the Rajah's rule, and of carrying on the government of Mysore in their own name, and by their sole authority." There is nothing in the 4th Article that in the least resembles these terms. That Article of the Treaty simply empowered the British Government to assume the management of such "part or parts" of the Rajah's dominions as might be sufficient to supply funds for the Subsidy,

* Mysore Papers, p. 48.

"*whenever,*" and "*so long,*" as there should be "reason to apprehend a failure in the funds so destined." The powers of temporary management acquired by our Government under this Article, were hastily and harshly enforced by Lord William Bentinck,—on insufficient and erroneous grounds, according to his own candid admission,*—and since that time have been amplified far beyond the intentions and contrary to the instructions of that Governor-General and his two immediate successors, so that many apparent obstacles have now been raised against a return to native administration. And yet the British Government have never ventured to do what Sir John Lawrence inaccurately says they have done. They have never carried on the government in their own name. On the contrary, the official designation of the British officer at the head of the Mysore Commission, has always been that of "The Commissioner for the Government of the Territories of the Rajah of Mysore."†

In the same despatch from the Governor-General to the Secretary of State, dated the 31st August, 1864, the following words occur:—"By no act or promise, actual or constructive, have the British Government ever revived the Maharajah's forfeited rights, or given ground of hope that they would be revived."‡

The Governor-General's assertion that the Maharajah's rights were "forfeited," is quite unwarrantable, as we see from Lord William Bentinck's own words, quoted in this passage from Sir John Willoughby's Minute:—

"We have the explicit declaration of Lord William Bentinck himself, that the assumption of the administration of the Mysore Territory in 1831 was intended only as a temporary measure. In a Minute (dated 14th April 1834), commenting on the Report of a Commission appointed to investigate into the causes of disturbances which were the pretext for depriving the Rajah of the

* Mysore Reversion (2nd edition), p. 22-27.

† Thus the Foreign Secretary writes to the Commissioner on the 29th March, 1864: "The Governor-General in Council can allow of no change in the existing form of the administration, which, at the same time that it is well adapted to the best interests of the country, sufficiently consults the dignity of the Maharajah by having its head entitled, 'Commissioner for the Government of the Territories of His Highness the Maharajah of Mysore.'" Mysore Papers, p. 40.

‡ Mysore Papers, p. 48.

management of his country, Lord William Bentinck makes the following important admissions :—

"'The entire question hinges, I think, upon this consideration: Has the Company's Government assumed the management of the Mysore country on its own account, or is that country still managed for and on behalf of the Rajah? Is the Subsidiary Treaty of Mysore virtually cancelled, or is it still in full force?

"'The answer must decidedly be that the management has been assumed for and on behalf of the Rajah, and that the Treaty is in full force.'"*

Article V of the Subsidiary Treaty provides that the Governor-General shall "render to his Highness a true and faithful account of the revenues and produce of territories so assumed," and that "in no case whatever shall his Highness's actual receipt or annual income arising out of his territorial revenue" be less than a certain sum. How could the territorial revenue be his, and for what purpose could accounts be furnished to the Rajah, if his rights were to be forfeited, if his sovereignty were to cease in the event of this Article being enforced? Far from there having been any intimation or intention of forfeiture, the objects of the British interference, as declared to the Rajah by Lord William Bentinck, were "the preservation of the State of Mysore," and "the permanent prosperity of the Raj."†

In the same Minute Sir John Willoughby writes as follows :—"The present decision is in contradiction of the public records, which in a continuous stream indicate the intention to restore the administration of Mysore to its native rulers at some future but hitherto undefined period. The Maharajah has never ceased to urge his claim to the restoration of his sovereign rights, and until now has never been peremptorily refused. On the contrary, on more than one occasion, hopes have been held out to the Maharajah that restoration would ultimately be made to himself personally."

And he adds in a foot-note to this part of his Minute :—

"In the year 1844, he urged his appeal no less than five times; namely, 15th February, 10th April, 9th May, 11th August, and 7th September. He again appealed in June 1845, and again on the 8th August 1848, and lastly, and more urgently than ever, on the anticipated retirement of Sir Mark Cubbon, on the 23rd

* Mysore Papers, p. 26.

† Mysore Reversion (2nd edition), Appendix C.

February 1861. In these appeals the Maharajah asks many perplexing questions; such, for instance, as 'Who was to be the judge of when the conditions for restoration prescribed by the Court of Directors have been fulfilled? Had it ever been before heard, that because a Prince or individual had been in his youth extravagant, he should therefore be disinherited? Have not disturbances occurred in the Company's territories, as they have done in those of Mysore, without blame being imputed to the governing authorities? Have not the best and most upright of governments incurred, as he had done, debts? What proportion does my debt bear to the revenues of my country?' Finally, he strongly contends, and I think with success, that the original assumption of the administration of Mysore was not justified by the Treaty of 1799. *Vide*, in particular, his letters dated 7th June 1845, and 8th August 1848, in the last of which he claims the fulfilment of Lord Auckland's promises made in 1836."*

And Sir Henry Montgomery remarks in his Minute that "it is impossible to deny that it has throughout been the professed purpose of the Home authorities to restore to the Rajah the administration of the country, and that they regarded the direct management of it only as a temporary measure."† He also objects that in one paragraph of the Secretary of State's despatch, dated 17th July, 1863, "it is said that 'the state of the finances was such as to afford no security for the punctual payment of the Subsidy;' whereas, up to that very period the Subsidy had been paid punctually in advance, and Lord W. Bentinck had subsequently recorded his belief that it was at no time in jeopardy."‡

Mr. Prinsep, in his Minute adverse to the Rajah, falls into the very same error, and, still more strangely, selects the exact term which Lord William Bentinck had employed in a negative sense. Mr. Prinsep asserts, that "the strong measure of 1832" was required "for the security of the Subsidy, which was jeopardised".§ Lord William Bentinck expressly acknowledged that "the Subsidy was not in jeopardy."

Sir Henry Montgomery urges against the same despatch of the Secretary of State, that the harsh measure of totally superseding the Rajah's Government is justified by alleging

* Mysore Papers, 1866, p. 27.
† Ibid., 1866, p. 20.
‡ Ibid., p. 21.
§ Ibid., 1866, p. 89.

as facts the exaggerated stories which led to Lord William Bentinck's hasty action, but were disproved by the investigations of the Special Commission of Inquiry :—" Lord W. Bentinck's letter to the Rajah, written, as admitted subsequently by Lord W. Bentinck, when he had not made himself master of the subject, is quoted. In it, it is stated, 'that the greatest excesses were committed, and unparallelled cruelties were inflicted by your Highness's servants,' such allegations of cruelties having been shown to be untrue by the Committee's Report."*

This is only one instance of the unpleasant characteristic pervading all the official documents, that while not even a specious case can be stated against the legal rights of the Rajah and his adopted heir, without re-asserting the fictitious prerogative which Lord Canning publicly repudiated, it is equally impossible for any moral grounds to be alleged for rejecting the Rajah's claims without re-asserting those fictitious accusations against him which Lord William Bentinck regretted and retracted.

We are not surprised when a journal like the *Friend of India*, representing the Calcutta Civilians and the Calcutta shopkeepers, casts a random epithet or two, such as that of "tyrannical sensualist", at the Rajah of Mysore. Although Lord William Bentinck, after personal observation and inquiry, declared that the Rajah's disposition was "the reverse of tyrannical", that he believed his Highness was "in the highest degree intelligent and sensible", and would "make a good ruler in future",—although the slightest local research would convince even the *Friend* himself of the utter falsity of both his imputations,—we are too well accustomed to that style of discussion in the official and commercial circles which the *Friend of India* represents to feel any extraordinary indignation. At Calcutta it is always quite safe, and quite acceptable to an English audience, to call any Hindoo or Mussulman Prince a tyrant and a sensualist. The arrogance and prejudice of race and religion, the lust of patronage, and jealousy of any native pretensions, there reign rampant and triumphant. The *Friend of India* has no more claim to be considered as an organ of public opinion

* Mysore Papers, 1866, p. 21.

than the *Pawnbroker's Gazette*, but it may be very fairly considered as the organ of that powerful guild of professional administrators who are allowed to rule India, and whose influence affects extensively the public opinion of Great Britain as to Indian affairs. The intimate connection between the *Friend* and the Calcutta Secretariat* is so well known, its leading articles have so often sounded the first note of annexation, that even its most reckless calumnies, and its most improbable threats and prognostications against the minor States, have frequently struck terror into the hearts of our best allies and some of the best rulers in India.

We do not wonder, therefore, to encounter in the columns of the *Friend of India* a contemptuous, disingenuous, and unjudicial tone with reference to the position and claims of a native Prince, to see his character bespattered with random abuse, and his rights under treaty derided as mere matters of grace and favour, originating in temporary expediency and terminable at our own discretion.

When Mr. Bowring captiously taunts the Rajah with being "wavering, inconstant, and led away by trifles", because at the formal official communication of a message which the Rajah "had long ago learnt from other sources",† his Highness presumed "to talk jocosely"; when Mr. Bowring in two successive paragraphs (5 and 6) of a despatch, first announces the Rajah's demands that his adopted son should be recognised, that "Mysore should permanently remain a Native State", and "that a landed estate should be secured to some of his illegitimate grandchildren"—the very demands that effectually provided for all his relations and retainers,—and then immediately imputes to the Rajah "purely selfish" motives, and a total want of "anxiety about the future of his many dependants and retainers, or even of his numerous connections",‡ we may marvel at the blind carelessness with which the commentary is made to contra-

* Even more mischievous than the close tie between the *Friend of India* and the Calcutta Foreign Office, is the post of vantage occupied by its Editor as the Calcutta Correspondent of the *Times*, so that the sources of information are constantly poisoned at both fountain heads, in the metropolis of India and of the Empire.

† Mr. Bowring had himself privately communicated the message several months before the interview reported in his letter of the 18th February, 1864. (Mysore Papers, 1866, p. 36.) Mysore Reversion (2nd edition), p. 76.

‡ Mysore Papers, 1866, p. 37.

dict the text, but we are not much surprised at the peevish and contemptuous spirit betrayed by the Bengal Civilian.

Mr. Bowring is, doubtless, an excellent public servant and an honourable man, but he knows the objects and wishes of his official superiors, and cannot but sympathise with them; his own greatest success and distinction in life have consisted in his promotion to be Commissioner of Mysore, and he can hardly be expected to entertain with much complacency the notion of his functions not being permanent and indispensable. The more firmly he is conscious or convinced of his own ability and industry, the more must his personal and professional pride be outraged by the prospect of even a partial return to native government. And possibly the natural amiability of the Commissioner's temperament may have been slightly affected for the worse by the long and unsettled controversy as to the Rajah's claims having delayed and interrupted business, causing him much annoyance and throwing additional work upon his hands. The Governor-General, clearly quoting Mr. Bowring, writes to the Secretary of State:—"Such a discussion cannot benefit his Highness, while the tendency must be to unsettle the minds of the people, and to disturb the growing prosperity of the country."* This excessively official objection evinces just that irritation at the Rajah's unanswerable claims that might be expected.

We do not, then, find fault so much with Mr. Bowring's unfair and uncivil detraction, as with the toleration and apparent approval his despatches receive from the Government of India. The honour and dignity of Great Britain are committed to so great an extent to those hands, that it cannot be a matter of indifference to us when we see them turned to iniquity. But we are still in the atmosphere of Calcutta, and the Viceroy himself is a Bengal Civilian.

For my part it is not until I arrive at the despatches from the Home Government that my heart sinks a little. Even the Minutes by Mr. R. D. Mangles and Mr. H. T. Prinsep, both of them retired Bengal Civilians, do not astonish me. The official experience of Mr. Mangles never, I believe, extended beyond the precincts of the Presidency

* Mysore Papers, p. 54.

City. It is so natural for professional administrators to be deeply impressed with the transcendent blessings conferred by their own forms and regulations, and by the employment of their own friends and relatives in every imaginable office, that the efforts of all this class may be forgiven. But to my mind it is a most painful and ominous circumstance to see the same cold shade creeping over the home despatches; to find the Secretary of State, having deferred an explicit discussion and an absolute decision for a considerable time, reduced at last to adopt all the perversions and prevarications of Calcutta, to revive acknowledged calumnies, to reassert exploded fallacies.

Mr. R. D. Mangles in 1849 acted as the spokesman of the majority of the Court of Directors in sanctioning and approving the annexation of Sattara, the first step in that systematic policy of extinguishing our best friends which culminated in the confiscation of Oude, and a year later exploded in the fire of mutiny and rebellion. The minority of the Court on that occasion, each of whom recorded a written protest, would have been almost universally acknowledged at that time as the five most able and distinguished Directors,—Messrs. H. St. George Tucker, W. Leslie Melville, and J. Shepherd, General Caulfield, and Major Oliphant. And now when, after a respite of ten years, it is proposed to recommence the extinguishing process, Mr. Mangles once more appears as the spokesman of the majority, while the five most able and distinguished Members of the Indian Council,—Sir George Clerk, Sir John Willoughby, Sir Henry Montgomery, Sir Frederick Currie, and Captain Eastwick,—record their written protests against the measure. The parallel is remarkable. It can only be hoped that the result of this second conflict may be very different from that of the first; that noise and numbers may fail this time to get the better of history, logic, and morals.

The style adopted by Mr. Mangles in his Minutes is essentially noisy and boisterous, and owes all its effect to a certain audacity of assertion and invective. In his attempt to answer one of the weightiest arguments of his eminent colleagues, Sir George Clerk and Sir Frederick Currie, he professes to "*brush away a fallacy spun to ensnare the ignorant*;" he ridicules the Rajahs of Sattara and Mysore as "*mere puppets;*" the latter Prince was "the merest puppet," and "a nominal Rajah;" the State of Mysore always was and must be "a sham Principality," and he denounces in general "the treachery, sottishness, and imbecility of these puppet rulers." In short, he affords here, as he did in his too successful Minute on the Sattara succession, the most perfect illustration of the contemptuous spirit and the unjudicial disposition with which so many Englishmen, more especially if they have graduated in a Calcutta bureau, approach any claim of right on the part of a Hindoo Prince or community.

All the apparent force of Mr. Mangles's Minute is derived, as I shall show, from his loose and incorrect statement of facts, frequently amounting to a direct contradiction of the records before him, from the most cynical defiance of every dictate of good faith and public morals, and especially from his persistent reassertion of an imaginary prerogative, which after having been unjustly assumed during twelve years, the Government of India solemnly and publicly disclaimed in 1860, with the approval of the Secretary of State.

Mr. Mangles begins by "brushing away a fallacy, spun," as he says, "to ensnare the ignorant." He says :—

"Advantage has been taken upon this, as on former occasions, to raise an *argumentum ad invidiam,* for the purpose of misleading the general public into the erroneous persuasion, that to prohibit such an adoption as that proposed to be made by the Rajah of Mysore, is not merely an act of temporal injustice, but a grievous injury extending beyond the grave, and an outrage upon the religious feelings of the whole Hindoo community; and this misrepresentation is the more mischievous, because it would be undeniably true if the British Government had really prohibited adoption, in the broad meaning of the term."*

The fallacy which Mr. Mangles professes to brush away is nothing more than a cobweb which he spins himself. Every one knows that although the term may conveniently be abbreviated into "the right of adoption," what is meant is the right of succession by adoption. Although we may very properly speak of the Government having prohibited an adoption, every one understands that what has been prohibited is the succession of an adopted son. To forbid a

* Mysore Papers, p. 83.

Hindoo Prince to adopt a son, would be as futile as to forbid him to marry or to beget a son ; to interdict a Rajah's widow from performing the brief and simple ceremony of adoption, would be as futile as to forbid the birth of a posthumous son. But to prohibit the succession of a son born in lawful wedlock, of an adopted son, or of a posthumous son, would be, in every case, and equally in each case, a prohibition utterly devoid of legal or historical warrant. It would be no consolation to a Hindoo family to be told, after their patrimony had been confiscated, that an adoption had not been really prohibited, "in the broad meaning of the term," that the funeral rites might still be duly performed, and that there had been no interference with religious observances. The complaint would be that succession had been refused to a lawful son and heir.

But although Mr. Mangles urges that for the due performance of a Hindoo's funeral ceremonies, "it is by no means necessary that his adopted son should be a Sovereign Prince",* it is not the less certain that the refusal of succession to a Prince's adopted son is "an outrage upon the religious feelings of the whole Hindoo community", because it amounts to an assertion of the legal nullity and inefficacy of an adoption, and proclaims the illegitimacy of an adopted son. Even Mr. Bowring, the Commissioner of Mysore, admits that "the feeling of all Hindoos, whether in Mysore or in any other part of India, on the subject of adoption, is deeply rooted."† The insult and the outrage are doubly embittered when the rejected heir represents an ancient and illustrious family, and when his rejection carries with it the extinction of a Hindoo State, the ruin of many local interests, and the downfall of a respectable and influential class.

There is literally no foundation whatever in Hindoo law or in the history of India for that distinction which Mr. Mangles attempts to draw between the succession to personal property and to a dependent Principality. Ever since the annexation of Sattara in 1848, Mr. Mangles and his school have been constantly defied to show some proof of such a distinction having ever existed, to adduce one single

* Mysore Papers, p. 84. † Ibid., p. 52.

precedent for the refusal to recognise an adoption, but they have remained silent. As Captain Eastwick remarks in his Minute :—

"It is a remarkable fact that, as far as I know, Lord Dalhousie, the originator of the policy of annexation on the plea of escheat, and its persistent upholder, has nowhere quoted any precedent for annexation in disregard of adoption, though he must no doubt have directed careful search for such precedents, which would have established his policy on something like a basis."*

Mr. Mangles does not hesitate to charge his distinguished friends with spinning a fallacy, "to ensnare the ignorant", and "for the purpose of misleading the general public",† and we have shown that this alleged fallacy is a mere verbal confusion of his own raising. But how shall we characterise the conduct of a judge or councillor who doggedly persists in referring to fictitious precedents, without attempting to produce them, in spite of repeated challenges from aggrieved appellants and dissentient colleagues?

It is still more sad to find the Home Government misled by the fictitious precedents invoked by Mr. Mangles. The Secretary of State in his despatch of 17th July, 1865, writes as follows :—

"In my Despatch to you, No. 45, of the 30th July, 1864, which conveyed my approval of the course you had adopted for carrying out the instructions contained in my letter of the 17th July, 1863, I merely remarked in paragraph 5, 'with regard to the question of adoption, I will only observe, that you could not recognise more than the Maharajah's right to adopt, so far as his private property is concerned'. I have now to convey to you expressly my concurrence with your Government in the arguments you have adduced against the Rajah's claim to do more than is above specified, and my approval of your having intimated to the Maharajah, that 'no authority to adopt a successor to the Raj of Mysore has ever been given him, and that no such power can now be conceded'."‡

The best answer to this extraordinary recurrence to the destructive prerogative disclaimed in Lord Canning's Adoption despatch, and to what are called the "arguments" by which the Governor-General, in his letter of the 5th May, 1865, reclaims that prerogative, will be found in this brief extract from Sir George Clerk's Minute :—

* Mysore Papers, p. 75. † Ibid., p. 83. ‡ Ibid., p. 71.

"This new doctrine regarding adoption is so novel and unjust, so opposed to all customs and religions in India, and so utterly inconsistent with the course of administration as previously exercised during the paramountry of Hindoos, Mohammedans and ourselves, that I can only conceive it to be the result of wild counsel prompting an indiscriminate gratification of a selfish policy which it is endeavoured to veil under a plea of expediency."*

But we will give some attention to Sir John Lawrence's "arguments." In paragraph 21 of the letter dated 5th May, 1865 (Mysore Papers, p. 59) this passage occurs:—

"Forced to acknowledge that in the time of the Mogul emperors it was customary for vassal Chiefs to obtain the assent of the Sovereign to adoptions for state succession, the Maharajah nevertheless does not hesitate to call in question, by the line of argument his Highness advances, the rights of the British Government to limit the issue of the adoption sunnuds to Chiefs who govern their own territories. His Highness bases his reasoning partly upon an assertion, the historical accuracy of which is not only open to be controverted by the facts of both Mahommedan and Mahratta supremacy, but upon which the history of the Maharajah's own family might have suggested to his Highness a comment, how far weak Hindoo Chiefs were allowed any discretion by Moslem conquerors."

The grammar and sense of the last sentence are somewhat obscure; but if we assume the most obvious and probable meaning, it is difficult to see how the Calcutta doctrines are advanced by it. We are not "Moslem conquerors." Moslem conquerors did not make treaties of perpetual friendship and alliance, "to be binding, by the blessing of God, as long as the sun and moon endure," with the "weak Hindoo Chiefs" whom they conquered. And, on the other hand, "the history of the Maharajah's own family" would only "suggest to his Highness" this "comment," that Hyder Ali, the "Moslem conqueror" who usurped the power of a "weak Hindoo Prince" without dethroning him, *did permit an adoption to take place*, when the present Rajah's father was chosen, as in the case of the recently adopted heir, from a distant branch of the royal family.†

As to what the Calcutta authorities say the Maharajah was "forced to acknowledge,"—that the sanction of the

* Mysore Papers, p. 71.

† Wilks's *History of Mysore*, vol. ii, p. 163.

Mogul Emperors to their adoption of a successor was always sought by dependent Princes,—the fact, though requiring much qualification, and doubtfully applicable to Princes with whom Treaties exist, may be fully admitted without injuring the Rajah's cause. The right of sanctioning and controlling a succession, even the right of investiture, does not, and never did in the days of "Mahommedan or Mahratta supremacy," involve the right of forbidding a succession. This is very clearly explained in Sir George Clerk's Minute.

"A fact well known to those of us who have been much in the way of observing the circumstances of adoptions of heirs to Chiefships, and to those who have made researches with a view to elucidate the subject, as Sir Henry Lawrence in the Kerowlee case in 1853, and Lord Canning on the general question in 1860, is that, if guided by the custom of the country and the practice of all our predecessors, our concern in adoptions consists only in adjusting the rival pretensions of two or more such heirs; a precaution which we and our predecessors have made it our duty to exercise in the interests of the peaceable public generally. Hence our sanction may in one sense be said to be necessary; for, naturally, a record of it is always sought by the rightful or by the successful claimant. Hence it is, too, that the confirmation has never been refused. Hence it is that I never found an instance on the old records at Delhi, and that I never knew one occurring within my experience of our own times, of any Chiefship, either Raj or Surdarree, great or small, being held to have escheated, excepting for felony, to the Paramount State."*

* Mysore Papers, p. 71. See also the *Empire in India*, "Adoption" and "Sattara." It is really too bad that we should have again and again to put to flight these mendacious phantoms, to attack those false positions which Lord Canning expressly abandoned. He writes thus in the Adoption Despatch, paragraph 19:—"It has been argued that the right to grant sanction implies the right to withhold it. This, however sound logically, is neither sound nor safe practically. The histories of feudal Governments furnish abundant examples of long established privileges habitually renewed as acts of grace from the Paramount Powers, but which those Powers have never thought of refusing for purposes of their own, or upon their own judgment alone."

And in paragraphs 17 and 18 he says:—

"We have not shown, so far as I can find, a single instance in which adoption by a Sovereign Prince has been invalidated by a refusal of assent from the Paramount Power." "I venture to think that no such instance can be adduced." "I believe that there is no example of any Hindoo State, whether in Rajpootana or elsewhere, lapsing to the Paramount Power by reason of that Power withholding its assent to an adoption."

And yet Lord Canning was of course compelled to write cautiously, and to avoid directly condemning the past action of Government. It is irresistible to say of the Calcutta Secretariat:—"The dog returns to his vomit again, and the sow that was washed to her wallowing in the mire."

But the Governor-General proceeds thus :—"Further, it may be added that the principles of the Hindoo law of inheritance have no application to Chiefships; but, above all, none to those held under the conditions on which Mysore was conferred on his Highness." Now the principles of the Hindoo law of inheritance have application in India to everything that is heritable. It is not true that any special limitation was ever applied to the descent of Chiefships. Nor has the Governor-General attempted on this occasion to show how the Hindoo law of inheritance, which is the law of Mysore, and the main object of which is to prevent the extinction of families, can be inapplicable to the family of the Rajah of Mysore. Nor did Lord Dalhousie, or any of his school, ever attempt to show on any previous occasion how the Hindoo law of inheritance, which is the law of India, and by virtue of which every Hindoo subject can transmit to an adopted heir all his rights which are heritable, can be inapplicable to the dignity and possessions of a Hindoo Prince, who, although a tributary and dependent Ally of Her Majesty, cannot be properly included among the subjects of the British Crown. The rights, dignity, and possessions of a Sovereign in India, and throughout the world, are transmitted either by the ordinary law of the land or by some special law of royal succession. No special law, no special limitation is applicable to the Rajah's case. He is the Hindoo Sovereign of a Hindoo Principality.

But it is said that, "above all," the Hindoo law of inheritance has no application to Chiefships "held under the conditions on which Mysore was conferred" upon the Rajah. The conditions under which Mysore was conferred upon the Rajah are recorded in the two Treaties of 1799. There are no other conditions; and no Article or Clause of those Treaties institutes any new or special law of succession, impugns or limits the operation of the Hindoo law, or declares it to have become inapplicable to a family whose successions had been regulated by its principles for many centuries.

It is very questionable whether the State of Mysore, bound to the British Government by a Treaty of perpetual friendship and alliance, can be rightly classed among "Chiefships." It is frequently termed the Kingdom of

Mysore by the Marquis Wellesley, the Duke of Wellington, and many subsequent Indian statesmen; and at the present day the Rajah is one of the few Princes of India, who sits upon a throne, and who is entitled to a royal salute of twenty-one guns. Were it not for the incessant efforts to damage the Rajah's position by depreciatory epithets, these would be matters of little or no weight, points rather of form and courtesy than of serious import; for the pettiest Hindoo Chief is really as much entitled to adopt a successor as the most exalted and ancient Maharajah.

After declaring that the Rajah's claim to adopt an heir to the State of Mysore ought not to be sanctioned, the Governor-General says:—

"The Maharajah is not a Sovereign Prince in the sense in which he uses the term; on the contrary, his Highness is a dependent Prince, having no rights whatever beyond those conferred upon him by the Subsidiary Treaty, and no power or authority to amplify those rights beyond the strict letter of the Treaty. That Treaty was a purely personal one with the Maharajah, and conveyed no authority to adopt, and made no mention whatever of heirs."*

The Maharajah "uses the term" Sovereign Prince in its ordinary "sense." In what sense does the Governor-General maintain that it ought to be used by his Highness? The Governor-General would perhaps reply, in the immediately succeeding words of this passage, that "on the contrary his Highness is a dependent Prince," as if the two terms were inconsistent and contradictory, whereas they are quite compatible. Any work on International Law will explain that a Sovereign Prince may also be a dependent Prince. But in fact all the attributes and titles of sovereignty were attached to the Rajah of Mysore in the transactions and Treaties of 1799, 1803, and 1807; and Lord Canning when Viceroy of India, so late as 30th March 1860, simply renewed a continuous recognition when he observed, in his despatch to the Secretary of State, that his Highness was "the Sovereign of Mysore," and that the people of Mysore were "his subjects."†

Captain Eastwick observes on this point:—

"With regard to the Maharajah not being a Sovereign Prince,

* Mysore Papers, p. 60. † *Mysore Reversion* (2nd edit.), p. 54.

we have never discovered this until lately. It is only since the absorption of Mysore has been contemplated, that we have changed our style of address to the Maharajah, and have adopted language more convenient for our purposes. Up to a very recent date, the sovereignty of the Maharajah has been uninterruptedly acknowledged by the representatives of the British Government and by the Home Authorities."*

Having thus endeavoured to cast a shade of doubt and confusion over the Rajah's sovereignty, the Governor-General then proceeds to say that his Highness has "*no rights beyond those conferred on him by the Subsidiary Treaty.*" Here we have the indispensable misstatement of the transactions of 1799, without which it would be impossible to degrade the Sovereign of Mysore into a mere tenant for life or during good behaviour, at the discretion of the British Government. The despatch speaks of "*rights conferred upon the Rajah by the Subsidiary Treaty.*" No rights whatever were conferred upon the Rajah by the Subsidiary Treaty, except—strange to say!—that right of calling for the aid of British troops, the exercise of which, although so clearly contemplated and anticipated when the Treaty was concluded, is now both cast in his teeth as an extraordinary boon, and made the chief pretext for his permanent supersession. With this singular exception, nothing whatever is conferred upon the Rajah by the Subsidiary Treaty. I challenge any one to read the Treaty through from beginning to end, and to find one word in the Preamble, or in any one of the Articles, which purports to grant or to concede *anything* to the Rajah. Everything settled by the Subsidiary Treaty is for the benefit of the East India Company.

Sir John Lawrence in his letter to the Rajah of the 5th May, 1865,† makes the same misstatement—a misstatement, as I have just remarked, which is indispensable for his object. He says:—"The Nizam was not even admitted as a party to the Subsidiary Treaty which effected the cession of Mysore to your Highness." The cession of Mysore was not effected by the Subsidiary Treaty, but by the Partition Treaty. It is expressly stated in Article V of the Subsidiary Treaty that his Highness's "territories"

* Mysore Papers, p. 76.

* Ibid., p. 69.

were "ceded to him by the Fifth Article of the Treaty of Mysore" (the Partition Treaty).

Nothing was ever conferred upon the Rajah by the East India Company acting alone. Whatever was conferred upon the Rajah of Mysore in 1799 was conferred by the Partition Treaty between the East India Company and the Nizam. And not only is nothing conferred, ceded, or granted in the Subsidiary Treaty, but not one single district or village that had been conferred upon the Rajah in the Treaty of Partition is even specified or named in the Subsidiary Treaty. In the Preamble and in several of the Articles a simple reference is made to the Partition Treaty with the Nizam as the document containing both full authority and full particulars. Indeed, the Partition Treaty is cited in Article XV of the Subsidiary Treaty, as constituting the sufficient title to the districts therein "declared to belong respectively to the English Company and to his Highness." Both parties are referred to the Treaty with the Nizam as the ultimate record. And in Article XIII, which contemplates a commercial Treaty between the Company and the Rajah, mention is made of "their respective dominions," and of "the subjects of both Governments." In Article XIV there is a stipulation "for the mutual welfare of both States." It is thus impossible to deny that the Rajah is a Sovereign Prince, in every sense of the term; and it is equally impossible to separate the two Treaties of 1799.

When the Subsidiary Treaty was about to be concluded, the cession of territory to form the restored Principality, "under a descendant of the ancient Rajahs of Mysore," and to be "a separate Government, as long as the sun and moon endure," had been already effected by the Partition Treaty; and by its ninth Article a Subsidiary Force, for "the effectual establishment" of the Rajah's Government was to be furnished by the Company, "according to the terms of a separate Treaty to be immediately concluded" with the Rajah.

The Subsidiary Treaty is simply supplementary to the Partition Treaty—"ancillary" and "subordinate," as was rashly acknowledged in the memorable Calcutta Letter of

11th March, 1862.* It declares itself in the Preamble to be concluded "in order to carry out the stipulations" of the Partition Treaty with the Nizam, and "*to increase and strengthen the friendship subsisting between the English East India Company and the Maharajah,*"—words which in themselves sufficiently indicate that the Rajah's restoration to the position of a reigning Sovereign was the foregone cause and not the consequence of the Subsidiary Treaty.

The dates of the two Treaties, compared with the time and incidents of the Rajah's installation, prove clearly that the cession of territory to his Highness, and the recognition of his sovereignty, took effect from the joint action of the Allies, and were quite unconnected with the Subsidiary Treaty. The Partition Treaty is dated the 22nd June, 1799. The Rajah was enthroned on the 30th June—his right hand being taken by Lord Harris, the British Commander-in-Chief, and his left by Meer Allum, the Nizam's Plenipotentiary. The Subsidiary Treaty, to which the Nizam was not a party, was not signed till the 8th July, eight days after the Rajah's public inauguration, and was not ratified by Lord Wellesley till the 23rd July.†

The next assertion in the Governor-General's despatch of the 5th May, 1865, is that the Rajah has "no power or authority to amplify his rights beyond the strict letter of the Treaty." Certainly not—and no more has the other party to the Treaty. The Rajah, as we have seen, acquired no rights, possessions, or privileges from the Subsidiary Treaty; but he undertook certain obligations towards the East India Company, which have always been punctually and faithfully performed. The Company, on the other hand, did acquire certain rights from that Treaty; among others, the right to an annual Subsidy, and the right of securing its regular payment by authoritative counsel, and by temporary management in case of extremity. How those rights have been amplified; how the strict letter of the Treaty has been interpreted by the stronger party, I have endeavoured to show in the Mysore Reversion.

The Governor-General thus continues: "That Treaty was a purely personal one with the Maharajah, and conveyed

* Mysore Papers, p. 5. † Wellesley's Despatches, vol. ii, p. 85.

no authority to adopt, and made no mention whatever of heirs."

No Treaty concluded with any Hindoo Prince has ever conveyed an authority to adopt, because treaties of perpetual friendship and alliance between two States never do include a law of succession applicable to one of them; and because until the year 1848,—when, as Sir George Clerk observes in his Minute, "the Calcutta Government led off with the barefaced appropriation of Sattara,"*—no one ever doubted that the only law of succession applicable to Hindoo Princes was the Hindoo law, the law of the land.

But the Governor-General says that the Subsidiary Treaty is merely "personal," and that it contains "no mention of heirs." The absence of the words "heirs and successors," becomes quite immaterial, and the notion of a personal or life grant becomes quite inconceivable, in the presence of the fact that this document is announced as "a Treaty of perpetual friendship and alliance," and contains a special formula implying perpetuity in the asseveration that all its provisions are to be binding "as long as the sun and moon shall endure."

But here Mr. Mangles comes to the rescue again. He says:—

> "I am aware, of course, that the Treaty contains the expression that, 'It shall be binding upon the contracting parties as long as the sun and moon shall endure,' but I need hardly tell any one well informed in regard to Oriental phraseology, that, strange as it may appear to us, these words certainly do not imply perpetuity to Indian minds."†

And then he quotes Sir Thomas Munro as to "the terms employed in such documents, or in Hindoo grants." The documents to which Sir Thomas Munro alluded were not treaties, but grants of land or charges on the revenue; and if Mr. Mangles were allowed to quote and to amplify a hundred arbitrary resumptions of estates and pensions by an Eastern despot, he would be no nearer a precedent for annulling a perpetual treaty of friendship and alliance. What does Mr. Mangles mean by talking about "Oriental phraseology," and "Indian minds," and "Hindoo grants?"

* Mysore Papers, p. 72. † Mysore Papers, p. 84.

The phraseology in question did not emanate from an Indian mind; nor does it occur in an Oriental document, or in a Hindoo grant, but in two British treaties, which were drafted in the English language, and every word of which was dictated by the Marquis Wellesley himself.

There really must be a lurking conviction in the minds of the most eager votaries of territorial extension, that there is something inconveniently sacred in the nature and essence of a Treaty, when we observe their evident aversion to a simple and straightforward use of the word, their efforts to avoid it altogether, to substitute some less solemn term, or to overlay it with contemptuous qualifications, even, at the last pinch, with inverted commas.* Thus Lord Dalhousie, when arguing for the annexation of Jhansi, pronounced the Treaty between "the two Governments", to be "a grant such as is issued by a Sovereign to a subject".† When the appropriation of Sattara was under discussion, Mr. R. D. Mangles, then one of the Directors of the East India Company, attempted to disguise the "Treaty of perpetual friendship" made with the Rajah, "his heirs and successors", under the insignificant term of an "agreement", and compared it with the grant of a sinecure office or pension.‡ And Mr. Willoughby, then a Member of Council at Bombay, whose Minute was mainly conducive to this first step in Lord Dalhousie's annexing career, insisted on the Principality of Sattara having been "gratuitously conferred" on the Rajah.§ In the same way when the question of the Nagpore succession was under consideration, Lord Dalhousie made a great point by asserting (most inaccurately) that "the sovereignty of Nagpore was bestowed as a gift" on the Rajah.

And Mr. R. D. Mangles, in his Minute against the claims of the Rajah of Mysore, calls the Subsidiary Treaty of 1799 "a deed of gift".‖

It is strange that any man, having any pretension to be a statesman, should consider it politic or dignified to depreciate the value of a British gift,—to indicate as distinctly

* As the Duke of Argyll does in his *India under Dalhousie and Canning*, (Longman, 1865,) reprinted with additions from the *Edinburgh Review*.

† *The Empire in India*, "Jhansi," p. 208. ‡ Ibid., p. 172.

§ Ibid., "Sattara," p. 169.

‖ Mysore Papers, 1866, p. 84.

as is done in the several instances, that the gifts of Great Britain confer an insecure and precarious title, and, even when confirmed by treaties, are less valid and less permanent than the grants of Delhi or Poonah! But, as I have just shown, there is no gift, of any sort, in the Subsidiary Treaty; and whatever was given to the Rajah in 1799 was given by the joint cession of the East India Company and the Nizam.

Mr. H. T. Prinsep, the only other Member of the majority in Council who has followed the example of Mr. Mangles by recording an argumentative Minute, has fallen into exactly the same mistake as his colleague. Mr. Mangles speaks of the Subsidiary Treaty as "a deed of gift". No form, or term, or word signifying a gift occurs in any part of that Treaty. And Mr. Prinsep says:—"A separate Treaty was made by the British Government with the Rajah of Mysore, to which the Nizam was no party, assigning the territory to him personally."* Now in the Subsidiary Treaty between the Rajah and the East India Company, to which the Nizam was not a party, nothing whatever is assigned to the Rajah, personally or otherwise. In that Treaty there is no cession or grant of territories, no assignment of districts, no definition of the frontiers and limits of the Mysore State; but reference is therein made to the cession and assignment of territories as having been already effected and recorded in the Partition Treaty with the Nizam, and one of his Schedules.

And on this point we are able to quote the direct testimony of the Marquis Wellesley himself, who speaks of the "country *assigned* to the Rajah of Mysore by the Partition Treaty".†

Mr. Mangles, having raised a dust round the question of adoption by brushing away a fallacy which no one has ever advanced, and flourishing once more his own fictitious law and precedent, five years after its public and official renunciation by Lord Canning,‡ then proceeds to argue that the Subsidiary Treaty of 1799 was intentionally made with the omission of the words "his heirs and successors", and that

* Mysore Papers, 1866, p. 88. † Wellesley's Despatches, vol. ii, p. 114.

‡ Lord Canning's Adoption Despatch of 30th April, and Sir Charles Wood's reply of 26th July, 1860, were both published in the *Calcutta Gazette*.

it was Lord Wellesley's intention "to leave his successors free to act, if the expectations with which the British Government made the experiment should be disappointed, as the circumstances of the case might demand".*

All that Mr. Mangles says as to Lord Wellesley's probable intentions, is the purest effort of imagination, and utterly at variance with all that statesman's recorded intentions. Mr. Mangles speaks of the reconstruction of the Mysore State "as an experiment",—an experiment to last as long as the sun and moon endure! Lord Wellesley speaks of it as "a settlement", as a "restoration", and not as an experiment,—as "the restoration of the ancient *family* of Mysore", not as a personal and experimental installation. In accordance with this view, and at Lord Wellesley's dictation, the Rajah is designated in the Partition Treaty as "a descendant of the ancient Rajahs of Mysore". In the same way Lord William Bentinck, in his letter to the Rajah of the 7th September, 1831, thus describes what was done in 1799:—"The sovereignty was restored to the *family* of the ancient Rajahs of the country, and your Highness was placed on the musnud." Not a trace of an experiment, or of a personal Treaty, is to be found in the Marquis Wellesley's papers, or in any official document before 1856, when Lord Dalhousie, in the full career of annexation, sounded the first note of menace against Mysore.

Mr. Mangles having failed to find a single word in the Marquis Wellesley's despatches, or in the records of that period, to strengthen his argument, endeavours to set up a case of antecedent improbability, or, as he puts it, impossibility, against anything more than an experiment having been intended, and immediately involves himself in a distinct contradiction of Lord Wellesley's avowed views. He says:—"The family of this child had long been deposed, and it had not the slightest claim upon the justice or generosity of the British Government."†

In the year 1799 the family had been deposed for exactly sixteen years; and even after their deposition by Tippoo, the British Government in 1782 had concluded a treaty with Cham Raj, father of the present Rajah.

* Mysore Papers, p. 84.

† Mysore Papers, p. 84.

"Between the British Government and this family," writes Lord Wellesley to the Court of Directors in his letter dated the 3rd of August, 1799, alluding to this Treaty, "an intercourse of friendship and kindness had subsisted in the most desperate crisis of their adverse fortunes."* He then refers to "the antiquity of their legitimate title", and observes that "*moral* considerations and sentiment of *generosity*, favoured the restoration of the ancient family of Mysore".

Contrast this with the assertion by Mr. Mangles that the family "had not the slightest claim upon the justice or generosity of the British Government".

And observe that Lord Wellesley in explaining his policy, never uses one expression that denotes what Mr. Mangles calls "ephemeral political expediency";† he even seems to avoid the use of terms implying a mere personal arrangement. He acknowledges the weight, without admitting the validity, of "the pretensions of the ancient house of the Rajahs of Mysore", and says that "no alternative remained, but to depose the dynasty which I found upon the throne" (Tippoo's) "or to confirm the Mahomedan usurpation, and with it the perpetual exclusion and degradation of the legitimate Hindoo Sovereigns of the country".‡

Undoubtedly he determined to make the Rajah so "dependant" on the East India Company, that all his "interests and resources might be absolutely identified with our own, and the Kingdom of Mysore, so long the source of calamity and alarm to the Carnatic, might become a new barrier of our defence".§ But he describes the transaction as the "restoration of the ancient *family*"; as "*their* elevation"; and observes that "by our support alone could *they* ever hope to be maintained upon the throne against the family of Tippoo Sultan".‖ He speaks of "the establishment of a Hindoo State", and of "a friendly and allied State in Mysore",¶ and declares it to be a "durable settlement". In short, a perfectly fair summary of Lord Wellesley's views is given by Captain W. J. Eastwick, in paragraph 26 of his Minute:—

* Wellesley's Despatches, vol. ii, p. 81.
† Mysore Papers, p. 86.
‡ Wellesley's Despatches, vol. ii, p. 78.
§ Ibid., p. 82.
‖ Ibid.
¶ Ibid., p. 99 and 100.

"Lord Wellesley re-established 'the Hindoo State' of Mysore, with definite political objects of high importance, irrespective of the person of the Maharajah. It was intended to make Mysore entirely subordinate as to foreign relations, and to preserve a command over its resources, but there is no condition in the Treaty, and no trace in the correspondence, of any intention to make it merely a personal treaty, or to provide for the lapse of the country to the British Government."*

Mr. Mangles having so completely misinterpreted the Marquis Wellesley's declared motives and objects, we may well refuse to accept his conjectural version of that great statesman's secret intentions. He says that Lord Wellesley was not likely to do "important business with so much haste and carelessness as to allow the accidental omission of the words 'heirs and successors' to pass without notice", and that in fact "it is quite impossible to believe that such an omission was accidental or devoid of a significant meaning".† But Mr. Mangles, unable to preserve a consistent line of reasoning through two consecutive paragraphs, does not perceive that Lord Wellesley, if incapable of overlooking a verbal omission in the Treaty, must have been even less capable of using the affirmative words, "to be binding as long as the sun and moon endure", without "a significant meaning". And the introduction of these words in a document declared to be a Treaty of perpetual friendship and alliance, renders the omission of the words heirs and successors a quite insignificant circumstance. This is the obvious verdict of common sense, as it is the unanimous and undisputed dictum of the authorities on International Law. Perpetual treaties are of course permanent and not personal. A "State", a "Government", when mentioned in a perpetual Treaty, signifies a sovereignty; and the contracting party to such a Treaty, who is said to have "dominions" and "subjects", is a Sovereign. A sovereignty is always hereditary, and a Sovereign always has heirs and successors.

I am quite willing to accept the opinion offered by Mr. Mangles that "no statesman was less likely than Lord Wellesley to do important business with haste and carelessness"; and therefore I think that if he had intended to make "a deed of gift", by way of experiment, as Mr.

* Mysore Papers, p. 77.

† Mysore Papers, p. 84.

Mangles most unwarrantably pretends, he would have made one, and not have made "a Treaty of perpetual friendship and alliance to be binding as long as the sun and moon endure".

In a later passage of his Minute Mr. Mangles says :—"It cannot surely be pretended that such a Treaty as that which Lord Wellesley dictated to the infant Rajah of Mysore ought to constrain us" to recognise his heir. What does Mr. Mangles mean by "*such* a Treaty"? He forces me to reiterate that it is a Treaty of perpetual friendship and alliance. What does he mean by referring to the undoubted fact that it was "dictated" by Lord Wellesley ?* Does he suppose that this dictation makes it less binding? I really believe he does, because I find the same idea expressed by the Duke of Argyll, who generally agrees with Mr. Mangles, and is indeed considerably indebted to that gentleman for the arguments in favour of annexation contained in his *India under Dalhousie and Canning*, reprinted (with additions) from the *Edinburgh Review*.† The Duke, who approves of all Lord Dalhousie's acquisitions and of the processes by which they were effected, and disapproves of the Queen's Proclamation of 1858, expresses great contempt for what he calls "the system of 'Treaties', which expressed nothing but the will of a Superior imposing on his Vassal so much as for the time it was thought expedient to require";‡ and throughout his two dissertations, when referring to our engagements with the Native Princes of India, he invariably places the word "Treaty" or "Treaties" between inverted commas. From his employing the expression "for the time", it may also be presumed that the Duke of Argyll cares as little for the word "perpetual" as Mr. Mangles.

* Lord Wellesley himself thus describes what took place :—"On the 8th June I had forwarded to the Commissioners the first draft of the Subsidiary Treaty, to be concluded between the Company and the Rajah of Mysore. After an ample discussion with the Commissioners, who had communicated the whole arrangement to the Brahmin Poorneah and conciliated his cooperation, and after the adoption of several alterations, this Treaty was executed in the fortress of Nuzzerbagh, near Seringapatam, by the Commissioners, and certain proxies on the part of the young Rajah, on the 8th of July, and ratified by me in Council on the 23rd of July, under the title of the Subsidiary Treaty of Seringapatam."—Wellesley's Despatches, vol. ii, p. 85.

† Longman and Co., 1865.

‡ India under Dalhousie and Canning (Longman, 1865), p. 11.

When the Duke writes of a Superior imposing treaties "for the time" on his Vassals, he falls into the common but quite inexcusable error of regarding the transactions of half a century ago as if the comparative power and reciprocal serviceableness of the Native States and of the British Government had been the same then as they are now. I believe his Grace very much underrates the actual power and influence for good or evil of the tributary and protected Princes at the present day; but even he would admit, on due consideration, that both the absolute and the relative strength of our own Government has enormously increased since 1799. At that time the faithful alliance and co-operation of the Nizam and other minor potentates were known to be of the highest importance to us, and were therefore much more assiduously cultivated than has of late been thought necessary. But gradually altered circumstances—altered partly in consequence of their continued and faithful co-operation —cannot convert our Allies into Vassals, change a Treaty of perpetual friendship between two contracting parties into a grant or deed of gift from a Superior, or justify the subsequent addition of inverted commas. And I must remind the Duke of Argyll that there were no inverted commas to the word "Treaties" in the Royal Proclamation of 1858.

But passing over with a renewed protest the Duke's unwarrantable application of the words "for the time", to engagements, which purport to be perpetual, it is surely very remarkable that his Grace, Mr. Mangles, and the Governor-General, Sir John Lawrence, should all, in their endeavours to depreciate the binding force of Treaties, lay so much stress on the fact, or alleged fact, of their having been "dictated" or "imposed" by the stronger upon the weaker party. This seems to be very like arguing that the stronger party who dictates terms is only bound to observe them "for the time", or for so long as may be "thought expedient". Because we were able to impose our own conditions, therefore we need not abide by them! This is very strange doctrine. We have heard the validity and permanence of a contract disputed on the ground of its having been extorted or imposed by compulsion;* but here we have that principle re-

*** Some of our Oriental Treaties might be impugned or protested against on that score; and we ourselves recently, and with justice, repudiated the Treaty with Bhootan, signed on compulsion by our Envoy, Mr. Ashley Eden.**

versed in favour of the stronger party, who, by the right of having used compulsion once, is only bound to observe the conditions of his own choice "for the time", or until he chooses to employ or to threaten another dose of compulsion.*

Sir Frederick Currie in his first Minute, dated 17th July 1863, dissenting from the despatch refusing to replace the Rajah at the head of his Government, makes the following remark :—"I think the decision impolitic, also, as likely to lead, when the permanent exclusion of the Maharajah from the possession of Mysore is promulgated, to inconvenient questions with the Nizam, whose treaty-rights in Mysore, though kept out of sight in this despatch, and the proceedings of Lords Dalhousie and Canning referred to in it, cannot be ignored."†

Nor was this inconvenient question long kept out of the discussion. The Rajah himself raised this very obvious objection in his letter to the Governor-General, Sir John Lawrence, of the 25th January 1865, printed among the Mysore Papers (p. 61). His Highness argues that the conquest of Tippoo's dominions was the joint conquest of the Company and the Nizam, that the cession to himself of his territories was the joint cession of the same parties, and that if those territories should ever "lapse," they would not lapse to the British Government, but to the Allies who shared in the conquests and arranged the partition of 1799. In paragraph 33 of his letter, the Rajah thus briefly sums up his position :—"I claim for my heirs the same rights as I shall have died possessed of; and should I have no heirs, then, for the first time, those who gave me my dominions will become absolutely entitled to them."‡

* The hideous cynicism of the following passage from the *Friend of India*, of the 25th of October 1860, has never perhaps been surpassed :—"Annexation is in abeyance for the hour, and it is right that Government should forswear all approach to it now. But the destiny of British power is in time to sweep the effete princelings who now rule Hyderabad, Gwalior, Indore, Guzerat, and Travancore off the face of the Peninsula." No Machiavellian precept has ever surpassed this unscrupulous proposal, that we should "*forswear*" for the present that policy which it is our destiny and our firm intention to accomplish "in time," or as soon as possible. Forswear annexation; swear eternal friendship; swear to respect treaties "*for the hour*," (the Duke of Argyll says "*for the time*,")—the pear is not ripe!

† Mysore Papers, p. 25.

‡ Ibid., p. 67.

If peremptory language and sweeping denials could overturn the embarrassing obstacle thus raised by the Rajah's remonstrances, it would have been effectually overturned by Sir John Lawrence's reply of the 5th May 1865. In this he says:—

"I must point out to your Highness that, in treating the conquest of Mysore as the joint conquest of the British Government and the Nizam, and the cession thereof as the joint cession of both parties, your Highness has allowed yourself to fall into an error which it is my duty to correct. The Nizam, at the time alluded to, was in the condition of a purely dependent ruler, and in a state of subordinate alliance with the British Government."*

The Rajah, in speaking of the joint conquest and joint cession of Mysore, has simply repeated the words of Lord Wellesley and of all the contemporary documents.

As to the Nizam having been "a dependent ruler" in 1799, it may be sufficient to reply that in 1853 Lord Dalhousie declared him to be "an independent Prince."† There is no foundation or pretext whatever in Indian history or diplomacy for asserting that the Nizam was either dependent or subordinate; unless, indeed, mere inferiority of material strength could degrade an ally into a position of dependence and subordination.

The Governor-General, pursuing and expanding the same argument in his despatch to the Secretary of State, also dated the 5th May, 1865, in which he forwards his correspondence with the Rajah, endeavours to make out the Nizam's subordination and dependence from the larger numbers of the British army engaged in the campaign, and from Lord Wellesley having exercised "plenary powers" throughout the expedition and in the settlement of the conquered territories. Sir John Lawrence omits to mention that the Nizam had specially conferred those plenary powers upon Lord Wellesley; he very much underrates the numbers of the Hyderabad troops that cooperated in the campaign, and seems to have overlooked entirely the large force of Irregular Cavalry, without whose aid our communications could not have been kept up, nor our supplies secured. It is not denied that the Nizam's own army co-

* Mysore Papers, p. 69. † Papers relating to the Nizam, 1854, p. 39.

operated in the conquest, but the Governor-General objects that it was not so large or so efficient as that of the Company, and that its movements were directed by British Officers. The relative numbers and efficiency of the two armies is really a matter of indifference. There is nothing unusual in the forces of one Ally being placed by mutual consent under the command of a General nominated by the other.

At various periods the troops of foreign States have been incorporated in a British Army; while at other times British forces have served under a foreign Commander-in-Chief. The army of Portugal during the Peninsular War, and a considerable Turkish force during the Crimean Campaign, were placed entirely under British officers. But I have never yet heard that such a military Convention impairs the independence or entails the subordination of any State, beyond the terms and purposes of the Convention, however small in extent that State may be, however weak in material resources.

The Governor-General thus continues his argument:—

"Lord Mornington with plenary power controlled the proceedings of the expedition. The conquest was therefore really a British one; and although from courtesy and views of expediency, the Nizam's Government was spoken of as conjoint in the operations against Tippoo, and was allowed to share with the British Government in the advantages accruing from the successful termination of the contest, yet such phraseology was conventional, and misled no one, and least of all the Nizam. For the Governor-General, whilst prepared to treat his subordinate Ally with the utmost liberality, resented any pretension at interference in or with his arrangements, and, dictating to the Nizam the terms of the Treaty of Mysore, intimated, with stringent plainness, that if the Nizam should object to the basis and fundamental principles of the Treaty, Lord Mornington was perfectly prepared to carry the new settlement into effect by the aid of British arms alone."*

Sir John Lawrence misrepresents Lord Wellesley's views when he says that "the conquest was really a British one." No such language was used at the time. The Nizam's share in the operations, and right to participate in the consequent advantages, though not rated equally with those of the Company, were never denied or despised.

Sir John Lawrence's argument is worth nothing, unless

* Mysore Papers, p. 55.

he means to say that because Lord Wellesley "dictated" the terms of the Partition Treaty, and was prepared, if necessary, "to carry the new settlement into effect by the aid of British arms," therefore Lord Wellesley's successor has a right to disregard the terms of Partition, and to break up the settlement for his own exclusive advantage.

Lord Wellesley, it is true, in order to secure his point at Hyderabad, instructed his representative at that Court to adopt a high tone, but at the same he acknowledged in the directions given to the Commissioners at Mysore, that if this adjustment could not be effected, the Nizam's claim to an equal partition would become irresistible, that there would be "no alternative but that of dividing the whole territory between the Allies."*

Although Lord Wellesley at the critical moments of negotiation, assumed an imperious and determined style in dealing with the Nizam, he well knew the immense value of his past and continued cooperation, and the impossibility of slighting his just pretensions. He writes as follows in one of those demi-official letters to Dundas, President of the Board of Control, which are certain to reveal his real sentiments :—

"I trust in God that before this time my brother Henry's arrival in England has satisfied your expectations respecting the settlement of Mysore. To have retained the whole territory for ourselves would have raised such a flame both at Hyderabad and Poonah, as could hardly have been extinguished without another war. Henry will have informed you of the difficulties which delayed even the settlement as ultimately effected at Hyderabad. The Nizam's pride would not have been satisfied without a considerable cession of territory."†

This is very different from the supercilious and overbearing tone which Sir John Lawrence assumes, and attributes to Lord Wellesley.

The Governor-General then flies to another fallacious argument, utterly inconclusive and irrelevant, even if it were not based, as it is, on the misquotation of a Treaty. He says :—

"So far from preferring any claims, such as his Highness the Maharajah seeks to suggest and to evoke in support of his own

* Wellesley's Despatches, vol. ii, p. 49.

† Ibid., vol. ii, p. 202-3.

pretensions, the Nizam afterwards ceded in perpetuity to the British Government, not only all the territories acquired under the Treaty of Seringapatam of 1792, and the Treaty of Mysore of 1799, but also whatever other territory he possessed, or was dependent on his Government South of the Toombuddra and the Kistna."*

It is not, perhaps, very important to remark—except as an illustration of the careless statements of fact which abound in the Calcutta despatches—that the Nizam, under Article VI of the Treaty of 1800, retained a portion of these acquisitions from Mysore, the districts of Copal, Gujjinderghur, and others, and still retains them.† But the Governor-General has not explained how these cessions and exchanges can touch either the sovereign rights of the Rajah of Mysore or the reversionary claims of the Nizam.

Not that the question to be decided is merely that of the Nizam's "reversionary claims," as the Calcutta despatches assume. The Nizam as yet has advanced no such claim. He does not wish to disturb the settlement made by the Partition Treaty of 1799, but he is not likely to admit the right of the other contracting party to disturb it; and the question is whether this ought to be done without his concurrence. The question of his reversionary claims would only be raised if such claims were advanced or enforced by the other contracting party.

In paragraph 14 of this same despatch from the Governor-General to the Secretary of State, we read:—"It has been shown that the acceptance of the Treaty of Mysore was a distinct admission on the part of the Nizam, that the sovereignty of Mysore rested with the British Government."‡ Nothing of the sort has been shown; on the contrary, the terms of the Partition Treaty of Mysore expressly negative any such view. There is not one single phrase or word in the Treaty that claims any superiority for the Honourable Company, or any exclusive share in the conquest or its fruits.

Far from "the sovereignty of Mysore" being admitted to rest with the British Government, the "sovereignty" of one very small portion of Mysore, the river island of Seringa-

* Mysore Papers, p. 56.
† *Collection of Treaties*, Calcutta, 1864 (Longman & Co.), vol. v, p. 71.
‡ Mysore Papers, p. 57.

patam, is expressly granted to the British Government by a distinct Article (III) of the Partition Treaty.*

At the end of the twenty-third paragraph of the same Despatch of the 5th May, 1865, the Maharajah is said to have been designated in the Partition Treaty with the Nizam as "the contemplated recipient at the hands of the British Commissioner of the Raj of Mysore."† And in the same way the Rajah himself was told in the letter from Calcutta, dated the 11th March, 1862, that in the Partition Treaty "your Highness was not otherwise a party concerned than as the notified future recipient of the liberality of the British Government."‡ These are complete misrepresentations: the Rajah is not once designated or notified in the Partition Treaty as the recipient of liberality or of anything "at the hands" of any "British Commissioner," or of the British Government.

Articles IV and V of the Partition Treaty are as follows:

"IV. A separate Government shall be established in Mysore; and for this purpose, it is stipulated and agreed, that the Maha Rajah Mysore Kishna Rajah Oodiaver Behauder, a descendant of the ancient Rajahs of Mysore, shall possess the territory hereinafter described, upon the conditions hereinafter mentioned.

"V. The contracting Powers mutually and severally agree, that the districts specified in Schedule C, hereunto annexed, shall be ceded to the said Maha Rajah Mysore Kishna Rajah, and shall form the separate Government of Mysore, upon the conditions hereinafter mentioned."§

Nothing in this Treaty is done by the British Government alone; the "rights of conquest" are exercised by "the Allies;" the cession is made "mutually and severally" by "the contracting Powers."

If we now turn to the Subsidiary Treaty with the Rajah, to which the Nizam was not a party, but which was concluded eight days, and ratified twenty-three days, after the Rajah had been placed on the throne by the Plenipotentiaries of the Company and the Nizam, we shall find that in Article V the Rajah's dominions are defined as "the territories ceded to him by the Fifth Article of the Treaty of Mysore," the Partition Treaty; and that in Article XV that Treaty is again mentioned as the authority, declaring the

* Mysore Reversion (2nd edition), p. 94. † Ibid., p. 60.
‡ Ibid., p. 5. § Appendix.

districts which "belong respectively to the English Company and to his Highness."

The cession was thus effected by the Partition Treaty. The Subsidiary Treaty, to which the Nizam was not a party, solely relates, as its name implies, and as its contents prove, to the conditions and securities of the British Subsidy, and to the relations between the two States. No cession is made by the Subsidiary Treaty,—on the contrary, it declares the cession to have been effected by the Partition Treaty,—no grant is made in it, except that of the Subsidy to the British Government. The Subsidiary Treaty, as was most inconsistently admitted in the Calcutta letter of the 11th March, 1862, is "ancillary and subordinate"* to the Partition Treaty, and is, in fact, inseparable from it.

It is erroneous, therefore, to represent, as the Governor-General does in his letters both to the Secretary of State and to the Rajah, that the cession of Mysore to the Rajah was effected by the Subsidiary Treaty, or that his Highness was the recipient of anything under that Treaty.

The Governor-General in his letter of the 5th May, 1865, impresses on the Rajah that "it was clearly understood by the Nizam that his accession of territorial rights was limited to the districts specifically assigned him in Schedule B of the Partition Treaty."† And in his despatch of the same date to the Secretary of State, Sir John Lawrence, referring to the transactions of 1799, observes :—

> "The Governor-General caused to be distinctly signified to the Nizam that if he elected to accept the Treaty, it was on the clear understanding, and the precise condition that his accession of territorial rights was limited to the districts specifically assigned to the Nizam in Schedule (B.) of the Treaty, and that the Nizam abjured all claim to the territory which the British Government was about to confer on the youthful Maharajah."‡

The frequently repeated mistake as to the British Government conferring territory on the Rajah, has already been sufficiently exposed. The British Government, acting alone, took nothing and conferred nothing. Whatever was conferred upon the Rajah was conferred by the Allies. And of course when the Allies conferred territory upon the

* Mysore Papers, p. 5. † Ibid., p. 69. ‡ Ibid., p. 56.

Rajah, to form "a separate Government," they *ipso facto* abjured all claim to it themselves. But there was no more abjuring, expressed or implied, on the part of the Nizam, than on the part of the Company.

It was, no doubt, clearly understood by the Nizam, that his accession of territorial rights was limited to the districts specifically assigned him in Schedule B of the Partition Treaty. But the territorial acquisitions of the East India Company were also limited to the districts specified in Schedule A, and to the fortress of Seringapatam and the small tract of land assigned by Article III ; while the provinces intended to form the separate Government of Mysore, and ceded to the Rajah, under Articles IV and V, are in like manner defined in Schedule C of the same Treaty.

The right of conquest empowered the Company and the Nizam to make a partition and settlement of the territories held by Tippoo. Whatever was acquired by the British Government, whatever was acquired by the Nizam, whatever was conferred upon the Rajah, are all clearly defined in the Partition Treaty. By that Treaty his sovereignty and his territories were conferred upon the Rajah ; by virtue of that Treaty he was enthroned by the Allies. Under the subsequent Subsidiary Treaty the British Government holds its annual Subsidy, its neglected prerogative of authoritative supervision, and its abused prerogative of temporary management.

We now come to deal with the question of policy ; and although Mr. Mangles seems to me to be equally unfair in his array of facts and equally wrong in his conclusions, as when he was arguing against the validity of Treaties, it is impossible to avoid respecting the convictions formed by him, and by the Calcutta Secretariat under successive Viceroys, as to the insuperable difficulty of restoring the Rajah to the head of the executive Government after thirty years of British administration. I have no doubt whatever that all of them have, in the words of Mr. Mangles, "an anxious regard for the interests of the great body of the people."* I think they very much overrate the difficulty and danger of the gradual transmutation of Mysore governed as a

* Mysore Papers, p. 87.

Non-Regulation Province into Mysore governed as a Reformed Native State; and I cannot but attribute these doubts and fears in a great measure to official and national prejudices and interests. But such doubts and fears most naturally arise, and deserve attentive consideration.

The Governor-General writes as follows to the Secretary of State in the Despatch of the 5th May, 1865 (paragraph 20):—

"There is no instance in which an administration, presided over by an organised executive establishment of British officers, has ever been under the direct power and control of a native ruler. His Highness asserts that, if the administration of the country were restored to him, it is not for one instant his intention to make any change in the present system, which would remain as it is now, a native administration, superintended and controlled in its every branch by English officers. Were this practicable, it is not clear what advantage would be derived from such a transfer."*

The Governor-General in alluding to "the direct power and control," "the power and administration of the Maharajah," adheres to the erroneous assumption that has so long pervaded all the doctrine and practice of the Calcutta Government with regard to native States,—the assumption that a Prince must either be a despot or a puppet. Mr. Mangles again is profuse with contempt for such "mere puppets in the hands of the British Government," as the Rajahs of Sattara and Mysore, "held in leading-strings" even when they were in charge of their own administration.† Would it then be such a terrible disaster for India if all the Native Princes were "held in leading-strings," and could become "mere puppets in the hands of the British Government"? In my humble opinion that would be a consummation devoutly to be wished for, enabling the Imperial Power to wield the immense influence of ancient and popular dynasties for purposes both of order and progress, to keep the peace without bayonets or cannon, and to improve the administration without superseding and degrading all the higher classes of the country. None of the annexationists seem capable of appreciating either the advantages of monarchy or the disadvantages of despotism. They

* Mysore Papers, p. 59.

† Ibid., p. 84.

never seem to have considered the utility or the possibility of a Native Prince being controlled by a Code of laws, and limited in his expenditure to a Privy Purse, under the watchful superintendence—not necessarily obtrusive or offensive—of a British Resident. Such a Prince would not, according to them, be "a real Sovereign;" he would be merely "a pageant Prince, a puppet, held in leading strings." They cannot contemplate or tolerate a constitutional and limited monarch in India; they will admit no alternative between a native despot and a British Commissioner.

Setting aside, then, this unnecessary supposition of absolute power in the Sovereign, the Governor-General is not quite right in saying that "there is no instance in which an administration, presided over by an organised executive establishment of British officers," has existed in a Native State, without the Prince being displaced or deprived of all share in the Government. There was something very like it introduced into the Nizam's dominions, when Sir Charles Metcalfe was Resident at Hyderabad, as described in the following extract from a recent publication:—

"Sir Charles Metcalfe, in the course of a few months after his arrival, discovered the total disorganisation into which every department of the State, but more particularly the revenue, had fallen before his appointment. He applied a prompt and efficient remedy by placing European officers as Superintendents in the different districts, who were entrusted with the general supervision of the subordinate officers employed by the Minister. The Nizam's Government entered into the scheme with the greatest readiness and seeming conviction of its expediency. The great object in view was to effect a general settlement of the land revenue throughout the Nizam's territories, and to afford the cultivators and other classes protection against oppression or extortion on the part of the Government or its agents. For this purpose the country was divided into several districts, to each of which was assigned an European officer charged with the general supervision of the revenue assessments and police. The executive, however, was still vested in the subordinate officers of the native Government.

"This system during the experience of eight years produced the happiest results, and the country in general enjoyed an immunity from oppression, and a state of repose to which for centuries past it had been a stranger."*

* *Our Faithful Ally, the Nizam*, by Capt. Hastings Fraser (Smith and Elder, 1865), p. 232.

And if, after the departure of that eminent man, the first opportunity was taken to discontinue this system of supervision and gradual improvement, it is but one instance of the utter indifference of the Calcutta officials to the internal and independent reforms of a Native Principality.

What the Rajah asked for was that the British official at the head of the administration of Mysore, should be called Resident instead of Commissioner, and should be, in fact, the Prime Minister of the country,—not, as Mr. Bowring and the Secretary to Government at Calcutta choose to misunderstand, that a separate and additional officer should be appointed, with concurrent jurisdiction, certain to lead to complications and inconvenience.* The Resident, at the head of the administration of Mysore, would be very much in the same position, though more firmly seated and armed with greater power, as Sir Charles Metcalfe was when Resident at Hyderabad with his staff of English Superintendents. The Rajah, like the Nizam, would be recognised and respected as the reigning Sovereign.

But the Despatch inquires :—"Were this practicable, it is not clear what advantage would be derived from such a transfer." There would be two advantages,—first, the maintenance of British honour, which is inestimable, even as an element of conservative strength ;—and second, the maintenance of a reformed and tributary Native State, of more value to us, in a political and military and even in a financial point of view, than a Province held in our immediate possession, of double its extent and revenue. The advantages to the people of Mysore and of all India, of maintaining a reformed native Sovereignty among them, I consider to be incalculably great.

The Governor-General then proceeds as follows :—

"His Highness must be well aware that it is a practical impossibility thus to transfer a body of British officers in civil employment, and a considerable number of European planters, and British-born subjects, and that the reversion of Mysore to the power and administration of the Maharajah is synonymous with the withdrawal of the European officers, and the abandonment of a system of upwards of thirty years' growth. It is

* Mysore Papers, p. 39 and 40.

tantamount to the collapse of order, and a rapid return to the state of confusion and of insecurity of life, honour, and property, from which, in 1831, the people of Mysore were rescued."*

All this inflammatory declamation is so devoid of a substantial basis, and is in some points so opposed to facts officially recorded, that it is difficult to acquit the writers entirely of disingenuous exaggeration. They write, no doubt, with the strongest belief that the Rajah's reinstatement would be impracticable and injurious; but it would really seem as if, relying on their good intentions, they felt themselves free from all responsibility for utterly unscrupulous rhetoric. Sir John Lawrence and his colleagues at Calcutta must know very well that the Mysore rebellion of 1830 was declared by the Special Commissioners of Inquiry, in their Report of 12th December, 1833, to have been "partly attributable to causes which were beyond the control of the Rajah's administration;" and that both by the Commissioners of Inquiry and by Lord William Bentinck, after his own strict local investigation, the Rajah was almost entirely acquitted of personal misconduct. The Calcutta officials must be well aware that Lord William Bentinck and his two immediate successors, Sir Charles Metcalfe and Lord Auckland, were quite ready and willing to replace the Rajah at the head of his own Government. The Rajah has pledged himself to maintain the laws and plan of administration approved by the British Government; and there is as little reason to doubt the Rajah's sincerity in giving that pledge, as there is to doubt the ample means and appliances at the disposal of the British Government to watch over and secure its due and exact observance. Well knowing, as the writers of this despatch do, the unrestricted power held by themselves to guide and control the Rajah, and to preserve the existing system unaltered, if thought necessary,—fully aware of the Rajah's willingness to accept the position of a constitutional Sovereign, with the Resident as his Minister, until such time as the Imperial Government should consider it safe and advisable to entrust more freedom of action to his Highness, or his successor, or to a native Minister,—it is quite inexcusable that they

* Mysore Papers, p. 59.

should profess to believe that the reinstatement of the Maharajah would be "synonymous with the withdrawal of the European officers, the abandonment of the present system, and the collapse of order."

The rhetoric of Mr. Mangles on this part of the question, as might be expected, is even more flagrantly unfair than that of the Calcutta Foreign Office.

"Let us assume," says he, "for the sake of argument, that the remonstrances of those who insist with so much earnestness that justice and the faith of treaties should constrain us to allow the Rajah to adopt a successor were permitted to prevail. There would then be two, and only two, courses open to us; either the adopted son must be permitted to become *the actual ruler* of his country, to appoint his own officers, *and to administer justice and the revenue according to his own views and principles*, or affairs must be carried on, as at present, by a British Commissioner, assisted by a body of British officers, who would exercise all real power, and in whose hands the *nominal Rajah* would be the *merest puppet*."*

Let me draw attention to the words which I have placed in italics. The "actual ruler" is of course the inevitable despot, uncontrolled and unimprovable. The "nominal Rajah" and "merest puppet" is that contemptible character a constitutional Sovereign. Why must a Rajah placed at the head of a reformed government, "administer justice and the revenue according to his own views and principles"? Why should he not administer justice and the revenue according to *our* views and principles, as the Rajahs of Travancore and Kolapore—no thanks to the Calcutta Foreign Office,—have learned to do? If Mr. Mangles and Sir John Lawrence do not know perfectly well that all the advantages of the present administration of Mysore could be naturalised and perpetuated under a restored native Government, then they are grossly ignorant of the happiest and most hopeful results of our political operations in India, and blind to the administrative ability—sufficient though not superabundant—which lies at their disposal. If, instead of hunting after imaginary prece-

* Mysore Papers, p. 85.

dents for ignoring adoptions, counting them before they have caught them, and constructing out of them a fictitious law of confiscation, they would turn their attention—for no research is required—to the real precedents for reforming Principalities, they would find that the "schemes, which Mr. Mangles pretends have ended in "utter and hopeless shipwreck,"*—the "experiments" which the Governor-General declares must be "futile and pernicious,"† *have never failed.*

It would be useless at this time to enter into any discussion as to the alleged ingratitude and plots of the Rajah of Sattara, which Mr. Mangles rakes up for the occasion.‡

I myself believe that all that Prince's misfortunes were caused by a Palace conspiracy, of which, in the words of Mr. Forbes, one of the Court of Directors, we were "the dupes" and he was "the victim."§ Suffice it to say that four of the Directors of the East India Company, Messrs. H. St. George Tucker, Cotton, Shepherd, and Forbes, recorded Minutes of dissent against his deposition; that Mr. Henry Shakespear, a Member of the Supreme Council of India, considered that "no charge of a serious nature had been substantiated against the Rajah;"|| and that many other competent judges at the time expressed opinions equally decided in favour of the Rajah's cause. And there is at least this presumptive proof of his innocence, that he steadily rejected all compromise, and when a full amnesty was offered him, resolved to sacrifice his throne, to abandon his treasures, to relinquish his home, and to go into exile with his family to a distant part of India, rather than subscribe certain articles which implied a confession of his criminality. "Guilt," said Mr. Tucker, "would have found it easy to accept the conditions proposed, in order to escape from the threatened penalty. The consciousness of rectitude must be strong when it impels a man to make a great sacrifice to a sense of honour, however mistaken."¶ And in this instance the sacrifice was tremendous, and was made with perfect deliberation and great dignity.

Mr. Mangles has used the supposed treachery of the Rajah

* Mysore Papers, p. 87. † Ibid., p. 59 ‡ Ibid., p. 85, 86.
§ Sattara Papers, 1843, p. 1260. || Ibid., p. 1255.
¶ Ibid., p. 1258.

of Sattara once before, with complete success, as a plea for the extinction of that State, at the death of the Ex-Rajah's brother. He may well be satisfied with that exploit, for he not only carried his point then, but he thereby fabricated the sole precedent for the annexations of Jhansi and Nagpore. I have but a few words to add on this subject. Mr. Mangles thinks that by maintaining a native Sovereign in Mysore we run the risk of future intrigues and doubtful allegiance. It may be so. Let us consider the guilt of the Rajah of Sattara to have been as clear as day. Then during his reign we had one disaffected and intriguing tributary. Is it equally certain that we had one less when the Principality was abolished? I believe, on the contrary, that by that unjust, useless, and unprofitable acquisition we created hundreds of enemies, and excited innumerable intrigues and conspiracies. Bad news travels apace, and travels afar. Sir John Low tells us that "the confidence of our native allies was a good deal shaken by the annexation of Sattara", and that it roused feelings of discontent and alarm throughout Malwa and Rajpootana, where he was at that time Agent to the Governor General.*

Mr. Mangles, though from his position at the India Office he ought to know better, may still be under the same delusion as the Duke of Argyll, who as a Cabinet Minister might have had access to the best information, that "the infection of the mutiny never reached the Presidencies of Madras or of Bombay," and that "the entire armies of Bombay and of Madras escaped the plague."† The Field Forces that were actively engaged for so many months in suppressing insurrection, not without much bloodshed, in the Satpoora district, on the Goa frontier, in Kolapore, Nargoond, Shorapore, Jumkhundee, and Kopal, and other parts of the Mahratta country; the mutinies of the 27th Bombay Native Infantry at Kolapore, where some of their officers were murdered, of the 21st at Kurrachee,‡ and the partial misconduct of the 2nd and 3rd Bombay Cavalry at Neemuch and Nusseerabad; the disaffection and plots

* Papers relating to the Rajah of Berar, 1854, p. 43.

† *India under Dalhousie and Canning*, (Longman & Co.), 1865, p. 118 and 92.

‡ Both of these regiments were disbanded, and their numbers struck out of the Army List.

among the 10th and 11th Native Infantry, in the city of Bombay itself, when two sepoys were blown from guns, and others transported; the notorious conspiracies throughout the Deccan; the sixteen executions at Sattara, several at Belgaum, and twenty-six in Nagpore,* might suggest even to Mr. Mangles and the Duke of Argyll some little doubt whether the disappearance of the Rajahs of Sattara and Nagpore from the political scene of India, did actually reduce the number or lessen the probability of hostile intrigues, or whether it did not rather add to and augment their number and their incentives.

And, therefore, while Mr. Mangles adduces for the second time in his career as an Indian statesman, the alleged plots of the Rajah of Sattara, for the purpose of crying down native dependencies, as if by abolishing the Mysore Raj we should be relieved from at least one chance of princely treachery, I shall retain the opinion, shared by many more competent and more entitled to speak than myself, that if that great injustice should really be perpetrated, those chances would be infinitely multiplied, and that in exchange for the one good friend whom we throw away, we should engender a hundred enemies, and justify their enmity.

Mr. Mangles has been very dexterous,—I might say ambidextrous,—in the treatment of his two illustrations. He heightens the tints of both pictures, and then produces the highest effect by their alternate exhibition. At the same time he is very careful not to display the whole of either of them. Thus he draws away our attention to the alleged disloyalty of one of the Rajahs of Sattara, without alluding to his administration, because the State was always well governed. He dwells exclusively, and in exaggerated language, on the alleged misgovernment of Mysore, because the Rajah has always been conspicuously loyal.

* In the Province of Nagpore, without counting those killed in open rebellion or summarily hanged by military authority, there were nine executions in 1857 for high treason, and seventeen for mutiny. But amid the greater dangers and horrors further north, these trifles were little noticed. And it is very natural that those who did their best to promote the rapacious schemes which mainly caused the revolt, should shut their eyes to those facts which prove a general disaffection, and should speak of the great national movement of 1857-8 as a mere mutiny of Bengal Sepoys.

The administration of the deposed Rajah of Sattara was declared by the Court of Directors to be "a model to all native rulers."* The country was equally well governed by his younger brother, who was not possessed of half his abilities and energy, one instance among many that might be given, —though none ought to be required by a statesman imbued with constitutional principles,—that the good government of a well organised State is not entirely dependent on the talents and personal character of the monarch.

Sattara was well governed, because the administration was admirably constructed, and the Rajah carefully and judiciously instructed, by an excellent political officer, Captain Grant Duff,† whose name is still revered in the Mahratta country. Mysore was badly governed, because it was disgracefully neglected. In the year 1811 the Rajah, then sixteen years of age, having received merely an ordinary Hindoo education and utterly untrained in administrative affairs, was allowed to assume absolute power. In the year 1814, when the young Prince was nineteen years old, he was encouraged by the Government of Madras to resent and resist the advice of the British Resident. Sir Henry Montgomery writes as follows in his Dissent of the 13th July, 1863 :— "The Maharajah is declared to have failed to have fulfilled the conditions of the Subsidiary Treaty by neglecting the advice of the British Government, though it is well known and officially on record, that not only was no advice rendered, but that it was systematically and purposely withheld." And Sir Frederic Currie says :—"The conditions of the 14th Article of the Treaty the British Government had themselves, it must be admitted, 'failed to fulfil,' when they systematically withheld from the Rajah the advice which, by that Article, they are bound to give him in the conduct of every detailed department of the administration. The withholding of that advice, and the withdrawal of the support of the British representative, with their results, are forcibly remarked on by the Commissioners in their Report as to the causes of the rebellion which led to the proceedings adopted by Lord W. Bentinck in 1831."‡

* Sattara Papers, 1843, p. 1268.

† Author of the *History of the Mahrattas* (Longman, 1826).

‡ Mysore Papers, p. 21-22.

the love and cheerful allegiance of the people and of the Mahratta Chieftains? Let Mr. Mangles turn to the records in the India Office and answer my first question, as to the financial gains; I can find a full answer to the others in those bloody events of 1857, to which I have just referred.

But why does Mr. Mangles term the existing administration of Mysore "a real government"? It appears to me that the British Commissioner is quite as much "in leading strings," which Mr. Mangles seems to think such a degrading and ridiculous position, as the Rajah of Travancore is, and as I should wish the Rajah of Mysore to be. Why does not Mr. Mangles either insist on despotic powers being conferred on Mr. Bowring, or deride him as a mere puppet, "devoid of political volition"?*

I am very far from admitting that the Rajah of Mysore ever was, or even that he is now devoid of political volition. However closely a Hindoo Prince may be held in leading strings,—whether his constitutional adviser be a Resident, a Dewan, or a Council of State,—he will always retain that political volition and influence which no British Commissioner can ever acquire. As I have said elsewhere:

"No Bengal Civilian, whether he be the 'highly distinguished' offspring of Haileybury, or the winner of untold 'marks' in open competition, can ever supply—even with twenty years experience—the twenty generations of the Mysore Raj."

"No British Commissioner or Governor can, on the extinction of a native Sovereignty, fill the Prince's place, exert the same influence, or wield the same moral authority. A certain moral force is destroyed, and physical force must supply the loss. The

ever, the absorption of small independent Principalities, which happen to be surrounded by our territories, will not always, in my opinion, tend to augment our power: on the contrary, it appears to me that such a policy would be apt to weaken it (except in special cases), by extending the British possessions beyond the limits to which our supervision could be safely and effectually afforded." (Sattara Papers, 1849, p. 86.) Yet when he was arguing for the annexation of Nagpore, Lord Dalhousie again began to urge the great advantage it would be "to absorb a separate military power," and "to combine our military strength." (Rajah of Berar Papers, 1854, p. 35, 36.) We required no European Regiment at Nagpore before the annexation; there is one there now besides Artillery. There was not a single British soldier in the Kingdom of Oude from 1846 to 1856, when it was annexed, including the period of our Sutlej and Punjaub wars, when every man was urgently required. We have now in the Province of Oude one Regiment of Dragoons, seven Batteries of Artillery, and four Battalions of Foot. And this is the way we consolidate our military strength!

* Mysore Papers, p. 86.

most energetic Commissioner would not undertake to govern Mysore without the constant support of British troops. More especially at any period of great national excitement—during an actual or impending invasion, or an extensive rebellion, led by a deposed Prince, a desperate pretender, or a religious fanatic,—a British Commissioner, though burdened with full responsibility, would be absolutely powerless unless backed by European soldiers."

"At such a time, when a British Commissioner without adequate military support, would be a laughing-stock, a victim, or a fugitive—a Hindoo or Mahomedan Prince, unaided by our troops, with or without the countenance and advice of a Resident, in the face of much local opposition, might, by lifting up his finger, preserve the peace, not merely in his own dominions, but over a large area of adjacent British territory; and would, to say the least, neutralise or impede a considerable part of the hostile resources, which, if unrestrained, would be arrayed against us."

Without going as far back as the eventful period between 1819 and 1825, when the Rajah, then in very loose leading strings, received the warmest acknowledgments of his "zealous and efficient assistance" from the Marquis of Hastings,—which having been repeated in an autograph despatch to the Court of Directors, can certainly not be treated as a mere conventional compliment,* we can find sufficient proof in the Blue-Book before us that the "political volition" of the Rajah of Mysore, now really reduced to the position of a "pageant Prince," was of essential service to our Government during the terrible crisis of 1857. In reply to the Governor-General's Circular, dated 26th February, 1858, requiring a report on the conduct of parties during the mutiny, Sir Mark Cubbon reported, that "the Brahminical caste (very powerful), even those in the actual employ of Government, were discontented and hostile; the heads of religious institutions, the great Sowcars, the petty Poligars and heads of villages, who subside with reluctance into their proper and ancient position of the wealthiest and most influential ryots of their respective neighbourhoods, are all against our rule, and disaffected towards the British Government." The Commissioner added: "In watching over such a community, there had been a constant call for information, and much had been obtained, proving beyond

* Mysore Papers, p. 34.

doubt the existence among the classes above named, of a spirit exceedingly hostile to the British Government; evinced in carrying on correspondence with the malcontents in the North, in the favourable reception of emissaries of mischief from that quarter; and in the convening of treasonable meetings at their own houses, for the purpose of plotting the subversion of our power." At this time, said Sir Mark Cubbon, in a letter to the Governor-General, dated 2nd June, 1860, "to no one was the Government more indebted for the preservation of tranquillity than to his Highness the Rajah, who displayed the most steadfast loyalty throughout the crisis; discountenancing everything in the shape of disaffection, and taking every opportunity to proclaim his perfect confidence in the stability of the English rule." And Sir Mark Cubbon declares that the Rajah's influence and the display of his friendly offices, "produced great moral effects throughout the country. In fact, there was nothing in his power which he did not do to manifest his fidelity to the British Government, and to discourage the unfriendly."*

Perhaps I can hardly expect to bring sudden conviction to the minds of Mr. Mangles and the Duke of Argyll; but I hope our leading statesmen, both Liberal and Conservative, will not remain blind, until it is too late, to the vast machinery of moral power, fitted to our hands and subject to our guidance, which the professional administrators of Calcutta are still sedulously bent on destroying. By twenty years of determined hostility to native States, these worse than Red Republicans, these Red Tape Republicans have gained promotion and swelled their patronage, but they have drained the military strength of the Empire almost to exhaustion, and have left us little else to rely on in India. Indeed, they seem every day more and more inclined to trust to nothing but material force. How much longer will British statesmen permit their hands to be tied in Europe and their faces blackened in Asia, by the officials of Calcutta and the retired officials of the India Office? Can they not think for themselves? Conservatives might be supposed to set some value on monarchical institutions; and Liberals

* Mysore Papers, p. 33.

ought to feel some compunction at the continued and extended degradation of an intelligent and docile people.

There is no reason that Mysore should become more of "a sham Principality" than it is at present; there is no necessity for any such degeneration. I hope for better things. Without recommending any hasty measures of change, and well understanding the prudence of very cautious alterations, both during the present Rajah's lifetime and during the minority of his successor, I can see no necessity for Mysore being for ever "administered exclusively by British officers."

Mr. Bowring, the present Commissioner of Mysore, has evinced an enlightened and disinterested desire to do equal justice to all his subordinate officials, without regard to race and creed, and with a sole view to the public good, by promoting—and I believe he is the only Provincial Lieutenant in India who has ventured on such a bold step,—a Brahmin gentleman, a native of Mysore, to the charge of a District, and by what he probably has found still more difficult, maintaining him in that position for two years.* I doubt very much whether this Brahmin gentleman is the only native servant of Government in Mysore or in India, who is fit for so high or even for a higher position. And if the reigning Rajah or his successor were again permitted to take a share in the executive government of the country, it is probable that the gradual introduction of well-qualified and educated natives into posts which have been hitherto exclusively reserved for English officers, might, by the Prince's influence and in deference to his natural prepossessions, be considerably accelerated. And this is the greatest reason of all that I wish to see the native monarchy substantially and not colourably restored. This is my greatest reason for deprecating any attempt to settle this question by a measure, however liberal, of compromise and compensation. I earnestly wish to save British honour in the face of the Princes and people of India,—I certainly do not underrate the urgency of that consideration,—but above all

* My attention was first drawn to this incident by seeing the appointment in the *Calcutta Gazette* of 3rd September, 1864; and I have lately ascertained that no change has taken place, though Mr. Bowring has been often importuned to remove the native in favour of an English officer.

I want to extend our means of usefulness. It is only by employing a native dynasty as our medium that we can arrive at the most satisfactory and durable result of our struggles and labours,—a reformed native State, organised on British principles, and never released from Imperial supervision, but governed and administered entirely by its own Prince and its own Statesmen and officials. The reformed institutions that are only to be found in our own immediate possessions, under the management of English officers, are superficial and precarious, and even while they seem to work smoothly, are maintained by a disproportionate waste of life and power on our side, and at a cruel cost of humiliation and political proscription to the most advanced and most improvable classes of the native community.

The most powerful arguments against renewed annexations seem to me to spring from the impossibility that all the varying interests and requirements of an immense continent, with nearly two hundred millions of inhabitants, speaking upwards of twenty distinct languages, can be adequately watched and tended by a centralised Government of salaried officials such as now attempts to rule all India by correspondence from Calcutta. Such a Government cannot continue for an indefinite period to command respect and obedience, or to be satisfactory and improving to the people in its action. The happiness and progress of nations do not depend on forms. The best institutions are not permanently safe unless they are under the custody of men who understand them, who have a personal interest in their security, and who are bound to the soil by the ties of blood and property. The system of governing India, in every district and in every detail, by Englishmen, is open to these fatal objections, that it lowers the moral influence of the Paramount Power, that it deprives of political privileges those among the natives who, with a little help and guidance, are fit to use them, while it does not educate for political life those who are as yet unfit. And the perpetual continuance and extension of such a system can only be plausibly justified on those grounds of utter contempt for the races to be governed which consign them to perfect stagnation, or incite them to privy conspiracy.

A more hopeful and a more progressive policy will never

be devised amidst the antipathies and antagonism and vested interests of Calcutta. It must originate here, and it is high time to make a beginning. Let us begin by abstaining from the unjust extinction of a reformed native State.

For it is not merely with a view to the Statics of the Empire, not merely as a guardian and guarantee of order, that we should maintain a Rajah of Mysore on the throne. We require him much more as an agent in the Dynamics of government, with a view to progress. The people will follow their leaders. We can never become popular leaders ourselves, but we can easily control, manage and direct those who are the natural leaders of the people. And here I must beg permission to quote myself once more:—

"We want a Hindoo Prince, such as the Rajah of Mysore, not to be an accomplished administrator, not to be a profound statesman, but to be the living symbol of authority and order, the visible and avowed representative of allegiance and obedience to Her Majesty's Imperial Crown, an indispensable connecting link and medium of communication between the Teacher and the Pupil.

"There cannot be a greater mistake than to set up that invidious comparison, which is so often made, between a British Commissioner and a Hindoo Sovereign. Their attributes and functions are quite distinct. With a native Prince on the throne, and in full possession of every befitting prerogative, all the influence of the British Government may be locally maintained in the person of a Resident, exercising with more or less stringency, according to time and circumstances, the right of authoritative counsel."

"Both as a conservative force and as a reforming agent throughout the Empire, the beneficial effects of a well-organised and well-affected Native State must ever be equally conspicuous. A British Resident, properly instructed, can bring all his representative and personal influence—either to preserve order or to promote reform—to bear upon the Sovereign and his Ministers, with whom he is in close communication, and who are connected by innumerable ties with all the great interests and centres of thought of the country, upon the most intelligent, the most deeply interested, and most influential personages in the State, upon six or eight persons who have the most to lose, and who know that they can be individually identified, and made to answer for their conduct. When these are gained the battle is won; but until they are gained, the British Instructor cannot hope to make a very deep or permanent impression upon the millions of an Indian Principality."

And let me once more call attention to the fact that British Instruction *has never failed.* It was eminently successful in Sattara, so much so that, while arguing against the recognition of the second Rajah's adopted son, Lord Dalhousie admitted "the excellence" of the deceased Prince's "administration," declaring it to have been "conspicuous for wisdom and mildness,"* and only expressing a doubt whether this was not attributable rather to "the personal qualities" of the Rajah than to "the nature of the institutions of the State." But, as we have just remarked, the State was equally well governed by the elder brother; and the greater part of the credit which on this occasion Lord Dalhousie was pleased to ascribe to a Hindoo Prince, was clearly due to Captain Grant Duff's instructions, and to the institutions which he established.

Sir Charles Metcalfe's reforms, carried out by English Superintendents, succeeded in Hyderabad;† but, unfortunately on the very first application of the young Nizam, Nasir-ood-Dowla, who came to the throne in 1829, the system of supervision was entirely discontinued, and the beneficial results of eight years' labour, prematurely checked, were almost thrown away.

In Nagpore, during the minority of the last Rajah, from 1818 to 1829, the efforts of Sir Richard Jenkins were most successful in introducing a regular plan of administration; and although many defects and abuses subsequently sprang up, owing to the neglect and total want of settled principles, which characterised our diplomatic relations with that State,‡ the good effects of British instruction were so far permanent, that during twenty-five years of purely native government, our active and open interference was never once required, to check oppression, to keep the peace, or to restore order.

The State of Travancore, now so noted for its prosperity and good government, was in the year 1808 in a much worse plight than Mysore was in 1831. There were no doubtful intrigues, as alleged against Sattara; there was no question of fiscal extortion, paralleled and even exceeded in British districts, as alleged against Mysore,—but there was open war

* Sattara Papers, 1849, p. 82. † Ante, p. 38.

‡ See the opinions expressed by Mr. Mansel, the last Resident at Mysore, Rajah of Berar Papers, 1854, p. 17.

against the Paramount Power, and utter disorganisation throughout the country. The Subsidy due to the Honourable Company had fallen into a long arrear; the Rajah, under the influence of an ambitious Minister, defied the injunctions of the Madras Government to reduce the number of his troops; the Resident's house was attacked, and an attempt made to murder him. One of the chief officers of the Court, the Minister's brother, treacherously induced a party of English soldiers to come on shore from a ship for refreshment, and had them all put to death. For several months the Rajah's troops resisted in the field the military measures that were adopted for his coercion. When the Travancore army was dispersed, the Minister committed suicide; his brother was taken prisoner and publicly executed; and the Rajah was reduced to submission. The disorders consequent on this insurrection were so difficult of repression, and a spirit of disaffection became so manifest throughout the country, that in 1809, under Article V of the Treaty of 1805 (identical with Article IV of the Subsidiary Treaty with the Rajah of Mysore,) the management of Travancore was assumed by the British Government. For five years full authority was exercised by Colonel John Munro, the Resident, as Dewan or Minister; and in 1814 on the accession of a young Rajah, the administration of the State was transferred to a native Dewan, extricated from its embarrassments, and in a condition of great prosperity.* The good effects of this period of British instruction have never been lost; the supervision of the Madras Government has never been withdrawn; and although neither the local administration nor the exercise of the Resident's influence has been uniformly irreproachable, on the whole the progress of Travancore has been steady and satisfactory. The Maharajah and the heir apparent,† his brother, Prince Rama Vurmah, both of them accomplished English scholars, are distinguished for their exemplary conduct, and their enlightened attention to public affairs and scientific pursuits. The Brahmin Minister of Travancore, Madava Rao, is a

* Thornton's *Gazetteer of India* (compiled by authority of the Court of Directors), article "Travancore."

† According to the law of succession in the Travancore family, the Rajah's brother has the first right of succession, and then the sister's son.

graduate of the Madras University. In special recognition of his merits as a ruler, the Rajah has lately received an augmentation of his titles and honours, and has been invested with the Star of India; while his able Minister has been deservedly admitted to the Companionship of the same Exalted Order.

The Mahratta Principalities of Kolapore and Sawunt Warree, within the frontiers of the Bombay Presidency, were placed under the control of English officers,—the former in 1845, the latter in 1838,—in both instances after a period of rebellion and disorder of a very formidable character, directly hostile to British power, and in the suppression of which large military forces were engaged for many months, and much blood was shed. And in both instances certain members of the Prince's family were implicated in conspiracies against our Government. Sawunt Warree is still retained under British management; but the Chief has received a *sunnud* from the Viceroy, assuring him that the adoption of a successor will be recognised in his family, should direct male issue fail. And in the mean time the Rajah's eldest son, who, scarcely emerged from boyhood, was engaged in the rebellion of 1844, and had taken refuge in the Portuguese settlement of Goa, has been restored to his forfeited birthright. This is a generous policy, by which we shall sooner or later gain more than the revenue of this little Raj is worth ten times told. But how strange a contrast it offers to the treatment of the Rajah of Mysore, upon whose fidelity or that of his family and adherents, no suspicion has ever been cast; during whose reign upwards of fifteen millions sterling have been paid as tribute; whose troops have constantly cooperated with ours on active service; who has been repeatedly thanked by several Viceroys, by the Secretary of State and by the Queen herself, for his friendly influence on our behalf and the ready and useful assistance rendered in time of need.

After having been entirely administered under British control for seventeen years, the State of Kolapore was restored to the rule of its Hindoo Sovereign in the year 1862. The results of this transfer may be estimated from the following extract of a speech made by Sir Bartle Frere, the present Governor of Bombay,* at a public Durbar held at Belgaum on the 28th November, 1865:—

"I had lately the pleasure of congratulating his Highness the Rajah of Kolapoor on having shown himself, after a long probation, worthy to resume the direct administration of his territories, which in the time of his predecessor and previous to his own coming of age, had, as you all know, so often been a prey to every form of misgovernment and confusion. I found his Highness not only himself able to converse in English with English gentlemen on most topics of public and private interest, but carefully training up under his own eye, and in his own palace, a class of young Chiefs, the sons of all the principal officers of his State, who will have the means of obtaining as good an English education as his Highness himself received under the paternal care of the Political Agents who have been Regents of his State, from Colonel Douglas Graham and Mr. Anderson to Mr. Havelock. I found every department of the State well superintended by his Highness in person, and every visible mark of justice being duly administered, and of the people being well governed, prosperous, and contented."

Surely this reform is deeper, this progress is more permanent, than anything that could have been effected if the Kolapore State had been appropriated, and had become a Collectorate of the Bombay Presidency.

Without adducing any more facts and illustrations, I think I may now claim to have made out my assertion that instead of any of our "experiments" having ended, as Mr. Mangles declares, in "utter and hopeless shipwreck," they *have never failed.* Wherever British instruction has been allowed a fair trial, it has invariably succeeded. It has never been allowed a fair trial in Hyderabad; it was relaxed too soon and too suddenly at Nagpore; it was never tried at all in Oude. In Mysore, after that disastrous and discreditable period of neglect and indifference, which the Governor-General terms "remonstrant forbearance," we interfered and introduced a regular and orderly adminstration;

* He was Resident at Sattara in 1848, and remonstrated against the annexation as much as was possible to an officer in that position. See Sattara Papers, 1849.

but thenceforward we unfortunately drifted into the opposite extreme from negligence. We have carried out certain reforms most effectually; but we have signalised our management by the complete and persistent exclusion of the Rajah from all share in the government; costly and superfluous establishments, entailing numerous lucrative offices for English gentlemen, have been imposed upon the country; and young Englishmen without any peculiar qualifications have been placed even in minor positions, the duties of which could be fulfilled in a much more efficient manner by natives, with the great advantage of their improvement in knowledge, in self-respect, and in attachment to British supremacy and Western institutions.

These errors were not committed in Travancore and Kolapore: those Principalities were not overrun with expensive establishments, out of all proportion with the requirements of the time and people; nor were appointments for young English gentlemen multiplied, to the detriment and degradation of native talent. The good work was done there,—as all our more celebrated tasks of pacification and organisation in India have been done,—by one or two able and experienced English officers in each State, with the aid of some special native agency, and the existing local authorities, so far as they were amenable to improvement. The large and growing revenue, affording so solid a basis for increased expenditure, may partly account for the progress of patronage in Mysore; but in the early stage of British management there was good cause for the introduction of a few more English officers than was at first contemplated, in the prejudices and passive obstruction of the older native officials whom we found installed in the districts. But nothing of the sort is now to be feared; no counteraction could possibly take place from any quarter; a large body of public servants have been trained in our system; and well qualified natives, educated in our schools and Universities, are available for employment. There is nothing now to prevent our Government from gradually restoring a native administration in Mysore. Mr. Bowring, the present Commissioner, as already noticed,* has shown us how easy

* Ante, p. 51.

it is to make a beginning; and if definite instructions and orders on the subject were given, and the work of reconstruction were entered upon in good faith and with a good will, it could be thoroughly completed in a very few years. The first and most essential step in the restorative process would be the public reinstatement of the Rajah at the head of his own Government, with a British Resident as his Minister.

So long as a considerable number of English officers were still engaged in the administration, it might fairly be considered advisable to maintain a provisional restraint over the executive action of the reigning Sovereign, unaccustomed as he must be to the forms and procedure of a limited monarchy. But I can see no reason why the young Prince, his adopted son, after receiving for fifteen or sixteen years those advantages of English education and political training, which—*pace* Mr. Mangles—*not* his father, but the Rajahs of Travancore and Kolapore, enjoyed, should not be admitted to the same freedom of action as those Princes, and, with the assistance of a native Minister, perform all the functions of a constitutional Sovereign.

There is still one somewhat plausible argument, advanced both in the despatches from Calcutta and in the Minute by Mr. Mangles, which must not be passed over without a reply. The Governor-General in that passage of the Despatch of the 5th May, 1865, which we last quoted (ante, p. 39), declares it to be "a practical impossibility" to transfer "a considerable number of European planters" to a a native Government. And Mr. Mangles expands the same objection in the following terms:—

"In another very important respect, the adopted son of the Rajah would find himself beset with difficulties which did not embarrass his predecessor, and with which, I apprehend, that no native ruler, even with the best abilities and intentions, could successfully cope. *Mysore is now full of European settlers, coffee planters and others, and every day is adding to their numbers.* If English magistrates find it no easy task to hold the balance even, and to keep the peace between the planters and ryots of Bengal, we might well expect that Mysore would be thrown into a state little short of civil war and anarchy, if native officials had to deal with differences carried on, probably with the same heat and pertinacity between the same classes with equally conflicting interests in that Principality."*

Now the term "a considerable number," is somewhat vague: I hardly think that a community of *five or six and thirty individuals* in a population of about four millions, ought to be called "a considerable number." But perhaps this is a specimen of what they call at Calcutta "conventional phraseology which can mislead no one."†

But Mr. Mangles employs no relative term, no vague expression, no conventional phraseology. He boldly declares that "Mysore is now *full of European settlers*, coffee-planters and others, and every day is adding to their numbers." As Mr. Mangles has immediate access to the best information on this subject, it is difficult to account for his having given utterance to this extravagant statement; and leaving him to explain the origin of his error, if he thinks it worth the trouble, I shall endeavour to show how the case really stands.

My figures are open to correction; but from the concurrent testimony of several gentlemen who have recently resided in Mysore, I have no doubt that the number of European planters in that State does not amount to forty, and is probably about five or six and thirty.‡ And the information that I have received is fully borne out by what can be gathered from the Administration Report of Mysore for 1862-63, the latest in my possession. Indeed, from the data there given, it seems doubtful whether the number of European planters can much exceed thirty. In paragraph 219 of the Report (p. 51), the number of acres held by Europeans is stated at 22,650, with the addition of 1,800

* Mysore Papers, p. 85. The italics are mine.

† "Such phraseology was conventional and misled no one, and least of all the Nizam." Ante, p. 31, Mysore Papers, p. 55.

‡ It is not worth while disputing about words; and this is not the occasion for entering fully on the question; but there are in fact no European "*settlers*" in Mysore or in India. The planters of coffee, tea, indigo, sugar, cotton and other valuable produce, are for the most part agents, or servants of mercantile houses at the Presidency Towns. Some, of course, are engaged on their own account and with their own capital; and in Mysore there are a few retired officers. But none of them have any intention of *settling* in India; none of them have any abiding place or permanent stake in the country; all are bent on making a fortune and going home as soon as possible. I know of one exception, and I have heard of another, but these are extraordinary phenomena; and who can answer for their sons? India can never become a Colony.

acres from the latest returns, making a total of 24,450. And in the next paragraph the average area of holdings is given as 933 acres for each European, one of them, Mr. Middleton, being said to occupy an estate of sixteen square miles. If, therefore, we divide the number of acres, 24,450, by the average area of each estate, we obtain the quotient 26; which I believe will give a greater approximation to the truth than can be derived from the Calcutta despatch or the Minute of Mr. Mangles. And without some better evidence than the conventional phraseology of the one, and the bold assertions of the other, I am not prepared to believe that there are more than between thirty and forty European planters residing in the Mysore territories. I should not be surprised to hear that the number is very much less.

By his wild statement that Mysore is "full of European settlers," Mr. Mangles not only gives a very erroneous notion of their number, but an equally erroneous notion of their location. Instead of being distributed over the country, as one would suppose from the phrase that "Mysore is full of European settlers," the planters are to be found only in two small corners, in the South-West of the Ashtagram Province contiguous to the Coorg Hills, and in the Baba Booden Hills, in the North-West of the Bednore or Nuggur Province, bordering on the Western Ghauts. If there were really any practical difficulty from the presence of thirty or forty European planters in a Native State, these small districts adjoining our frontiers, could easily be ceded by the Rajah, either with a corresponding deduction from the Subsidy, or in exchange for British territory.* For these hilly regions alone are suitable for coffee cultivation, which can never be extended beyond them, and their area is very limited.

Mr. Mangles having told us that Mysore is "full of European settlers", adds that "every day is adding to their numbers". If every day, or even every week added *one* to their numbers, the European planters of Mysore would long ere this have formed an important body. But notwithstanding the authority of Mr. Mangles,—and in his position he ought to know,—I am doubtful of a very rapid or continuous in-

* Some small interchanges of territory were effected by Treaty in 1804.

crease in their numbers. The Administration Report of 1862-63 (para. 220) tells us that at that time "the best land in most places had been taken up". We are told also that although the larger holdings are in the possession of Europeans, "the vast majority of grants are held by natives"; whose aggregate estates more than double those in European hands. And the latest returns from the Ashtagram Province referred to in paragraph 219 of the Report, show that 85 per cent. of the recent increase was in native holdings. From the latest information I am inclined to believe that the number of European planters is rather on the decrease. I have been told that the great success of the early planters consisted in their obtaining large grants on very favourable conditions, stocking them with coffee-trees, and disposing of their estates on terms which are not to be obtained now, when the actual profits are more clearly ascertained, and have, indeed, become, by the rise of wages in the Hills* and other circumstances, more equalised with those of ordinary agricultural enterprise—and thus it would appear that new grants of land are chiefly made to natives, content, as they are, with a more moderate rate of profits. The Commissioner informs us, in paragraph 222 of the Administration Report for 1862-63, that the provisions of these grants and their assessment have been several times relaxed for the relief of the coffee-planters; and that the tax levied at present, "although popular with Natives from its indirect incidence", is found to be "a heavy burden", and "is objected to by the European planters".

I believe that Mr. Bowring quite sums up the results and the future prospects of Mysore coffee-planting in paragraph 224 of the Report, in which he says that the English planters "have acted as pioneers in a new country,—a part of the country formerly considered as the least promising,—their undertaking has been shown to be successful, and the Natives of all classes are now awake to the value of land, and anxious for its possession". The original pioneers have reaped a well-deserved reward, and most of them have retired from the scene of their success; but I question very much whether the English coffee-planters in Mysore,—

* In Paragraph 224 of the Administration Report the rise of wages is mentioned.

though no doubt some are doing well,—form on the whole so prosperous and so contented a community at present, as to render any further increase in their number at all probable.

Perhaps Mr. Mangles, after having satisfied himself that Mysore is not yet quite full of English planters, that their number does not amount to forty among four millions, and that their numbers are not increasing "every day", might be induced to modify his views as to the insurmountable objections to their residence in a Native State. He may refer at his leisure to some other facts of a reassuring tendency. Travancore is a long way from Calcutta, and possibly even the Governor General and his Secretaries may not be aware that in the Hills of that Native State there are numerous coffee-plantations belonging to English gentlemen. The Dewan, in the Administration Report for the year 1864-65, states that about 24,312 acres have already been appropriated,—about one third of the area under coffee cultivation in Mysore,—and he remarks, (paragraphs 102 and 103, page 22, 23)

> "This enterprise promises to be the means of giving employment to many subjects of Travancore."
>
> "It is gratifying to state that the advantages held out to the labourer by this new field of industry are, so far as the experience hitherto acquired extends, quite unalloyed. All the planters are gentlemen sincerely solicitous to deal fairly with their labourers, and to rely upon good treatment and good wages alone for attracting labour."

He does not seem to anticipate that the introduction of British capital and enterprise into the Principality will produce anything like that "civil war and anarchy", which Mr. Mangles dreads; nor have I heard that the Resident at Travancore has expressed any apprehension of that sort. And yet in Travancore the "differences" and "conflicting interests", between the planters and the ryots, which Mr. Mangles looks upon as quite irreconcileable without our own elaborate forms, must be settled by "native officials" exclusively, for there are no others. If the views expressed by Mr. Mangles were accepted by our Government, they would be bound, as soon as Travancore became "full of European settlers," *i. e.*, when they reached the number of thirty-five,

—to watch eagerly, out of a regard for this new interest, for the first opportunity to annex Travancore. And if the doctrine of Mr. Mangles and Mr. Prinsep as to "a personal Treaty", were worth anything, we should not have long to wait. The demise of the reigning Rajah would serve our turn; for the Treaty of 1805, identical in almost every respect with the Subsidiary Treaty of 1799 with the Rajah of Mysore, is identical with it in having no mention of "heirs and successors." It is a Treaty between the East India Company and the Maharajah Ram Rajah Bahadoor, and is declared in the Preamble to be concluded "for himself."* It is true that it is to last "as long as the sun and moon endure," but Mr. Mangles tells us that is an insignificant form. It is true that a succession has taken place since it was concluded, but Mr. Prinsep assures us that is of no consequence.†

Not only are disputes between these planters and cultivating occupants settled by the native authorities in Travancore, but even in Mysore, under the existing administration, nearly all the differences between the planters and the ryots are actually disposed of by native officials, whose duties, it is true, are carried on subject to an appeal, and to the revision of English Superintendents. But this supervision and protection of the planters' interests, would equally exist if a native government under the Rajah were restored in Mysore. Mr. Mangles knows perfectly well, and so do the Civilians at Calcutta, that English planters and British born persons in a Native State are never made subject to the local magistrature in criminal matters, and only to a certain limited extent to the local civil jurisdiction; but that under special capitulations with the Native Princes, of which one was concluded with the Nizam in 1861,‡ the Resident is constituted the judge in crimes and disputes arising among Europeans and descendants of Europeans.

Many experienced persons, both among the planters and

* *Collection of Treaties*, Calcutta, 1864 (Longman and Co.), vol. v, p. 311.

† Mysore Papers, p. 90.

‡ *Collection of Treaties*, Calcutta, 1864 (Longman & Co., London), vol. v, p. 117. This concession was, I believe, made by the Nizam, chiefly on account of the Railway passing through his dominions.

the English official class, are of opinion that the interests and enterprise of a few scattered individuals of the dominant race can be much more effectually fostered, and their peculiar relations with the labouring occupants more fairly regulated, by a machinery like our Consular system in the East, than by that ostensible equality before the law which, as Mr. Mangles seems more than half to understand, has failed and still fails grievously to secure even-handed justice and good order in our own long settled Province of Bengal.

One thing is very certain, that the idea of a European planter or merchant being oppressed or persecuted by a native official, or even a Native Prince, or by a British Resident, is so utterly preposterous and incredible, that it will never meet with anything but ridicule from persons acquainted with life and manners in India. The independent and non-official Englishman belongs to a very visible and a very audible class. Even the Thugs never ventured to operate on a European.

It is clear, therefore, that either by the transfer of two small hilly districts to the British Government, or by about three dozen European planters being left subject to the judicial control of the same English official, under another designation, to whom they are now subject, the "practical impossibility" denounced by the Calcutta Government, would disappear. For it must be remembered that legally Mysore is still a foreign State, that British law cannot be administered there,* and that the Commissioner is the supreme authority over the English planters, as the Resident would be if the Rajah were reinstated.

Although I consider the question of right to have been adequately treated by me before I turned to that of policy, some remarks by Mr. Mangles towards the close of his Minute, compel me once more to revert to it. The Calcutta officials did not fail to perceive the obstruction offered by Lord Canning's Adoption Despatch, but they endeavour to remove it in the following fashion :—

"Nor, it is plain, can the Maharajah have any claim under the general right of adoption guaranteed by Lord Canning to Hindoo

* All these inconveniences, and even the difficulties arising from British process not running in a foreign State, could easily be remedied, partly by British legislation and partly by treaty with the native Princes.

Chiefs governing their own territories. For thirty years the Maharajah had ceased to govern; and while, in accordance with the expressed intention of Lord Canning's Despatch that the assurance should be conveyed to each Chief individually, a sunnud guaranteeing the right to adopt was granted to every Chief governing a State 'no matter how small,' a sunnud was advisedly withheld from the Maharajah of Mysore."*

Now the general plan and object of Lord Canning's circular may well be applauded, as a graceful retreat from an offensive and untenable position, but there are absolutely no grounds for maintaining that the Rajah of Mysore, or any other Hindoo Sovereign, ever had, or has now, any need of the Viceroy's permission, in any form, as the preliminary or as the ratification of a fully effective adoption. But even granting what is quite inadmissible, that it was legal or equitable to exclude Princes who were not then governing their own territories, it would, in the instance of the Rajah of Mysore, be taking advantage of our own wrong, to exclude him. For the strongest points of his appeal are that we were too hasty and sweeping in assuming the management of his country; and that we have retained the management in our hands long after the declared object has been attained, and far beyond what was contemplated by the Treaty.

There is no principle or consistency of purpose visible in the exclusion of the Rajah of Mysore; and it is impossible to believe that Lord Canning purposely, and with a hostile intention, gave him no written notice that his adoption would be recognised, when we observe that such a written notice was sent to the Rajahs of Kolapore† and Sawunt

* Mysore Papers, p. 48.

† Since the first part of these pages was printed, the news has arrived of the sudden death of the Rajah Sivajee of Kolapore on the 4th August. It is thus noticed in the *Times* of India:—" The announcement of the death of the Rajah of Kolapoor in the prime of life, and in the midst of many plans of usefulness for the well-being and advancement of his people, has been received with unfeigned regret by all classes in Western India, and many in England also will share in this regret. The Rajah was a representative of the younger branch of the House of Sivajee, the founder of the late Mahratta dynasty, whose name he bore, and was looked up to in the Deccan as the head of the Mahratta chiefs and nobility. He succeeded to the Kolapoor Principality in 1838 when quite a child, and a Council of Regency was formed to administer the country during his minority. The members of this Regency quarrelled among themselves, and by their misgovernment compelled the British Government to interfere. This was followed by an insurrection in 1844-5, which was

Warree, neither of whom, as already observed, were then "governing their own territories."

As to Lord Canning having "advisedly" withheld a sunnud from the Rajah, the Governor General and his Secretaries know perfectly well that Lord Canning did so, not from any doubt of the Rajah's right to adopt, but because he was labouring under the erroneous impression that the Rajah did not wish to adopt, and that therefore it would be equally impolitic and inconsiderate to encourage or urge him to take that step.* He clearly believed at that time that the Rajah and himself were both of one mind on the subject. Sir John Willoughby states as follows in one of his Minutes :—"By a comparison of dates, it seems to me clear that Lord Canning had no idea of excluding the Rajah from the benefits of his adoption policy by resorting to such a quibble as that the Rajah is not 'now governing his own territory'."†

On this point, however, Mr. Mangles says :—

"The name of the Rajah of Mysore is not found in those lists, and no sunnud was addressed to him. Can it be believed that these were accidental omissions, and that Lord Canning, if he had not forgotten for the time the existence of such a person, would have treated the Rajah on the same footing as the hereditary Princes of Rajpootana, or of what were formerly called 'the protected Sikh States'? I cannot give credit to such an hypothesis, and, therefore, I must believe that Lord Canning intentionally omitted the name of the Rajah of Mysore from the list of those to whom 'the assurance' of his Government was to be conveyed, because he was satisfied, as I am satisfied, that, under the circumstances of his case, he had no just or reasonable claim to the privilege in question."‡

But if Mr. Mangles is not aware of the fact, some of his

put down at considerable expense to the State. On the restoration of order the British Government assumed the entire administration of the country and placed it under the control of a political officer, to whom the care and education of the young Rajah was specially entrusted. During the mutinies the Rajah behaved with conspicuous fidelity, while his half-brother Chimna Sahib (now a state prisoner at Kurrachee) threw all his influence into the opposite scale. The loyal example of the Rajah, and his acknowledged fitness to rule, induced Her Majesty's Government, in 1862, to invest him with the management of his Principality. The Rajah's administration since this period has afforded many proofs of his being one of the most enlightened among the native Princes of Western India."

* *Mysore Reversion* (2nd edit.), p. 115.

† Mysore Papers, 1866, p. 31.

‡ Ibid., p. 86.

colleagues, and the two last Secretaries of State, are well aware that Lord Canning, though anxious to obtain Mysore by bequest from the Rajah (which in itself is a full admission of his Sovereignty), has left in writing the most distinct avowal that the Rajah's right of adopting a successor could not be disputed.

Mr. Prinsep, like Mr. Mangles, has "no doubt whatever" that the omission of the words "heirs and successors" in the Subsidiary Treaty was intentional on the part of the Marquis Wellesley. I have already shown that this omission could not have been intentional,* and that in "a perpetual Treaty to be binding as long as the sun and moon endure", such an omission is quite insignificant.† But Mr. Prinsep endeavours to prove Lord Wellesley's intention by adducing another case in which he supposes that statesman to have excluded the words "heirs and successors" from a Treaty, in order to convert it into a merely personal grant. And here he has only afforded one more instance of those misquotations of public documents and misstatements of officially recorded facts, without which it seems impossible to make even a semblance of assailing the Rajah's rights. He says:—"In the case of Arcot, this Governor-General specifically erased the words 'heirs and successors' from the Treaty with that Prince when it was sent up to him for approval and ratification."‡

Mr. Prinsep, a Member of the Council of India, with all the records at hand, is entirely wrong. The Governor-General did *not* "specifically erase" the words "heirs and successors" from the Treaty as sent up to be ratified; and he did not do so for the simple reason that those words were not in the Treaty. All that Lord Wellesley did was to have the word "established" substituted for the word "acknowledged". The passage in the original edition of the Treaty to which Lord Wellesley objected, had no reference to the future descent of the Nawab's dignity, but to his accession to the throne by "the hereditary right of his father, the Nawab Ameer-ool-Omrah Bahadoor." Instead of this right being "*acknowledged* by the East India Company," the new Preamble, drafted by Lord Wellesley, an-

* Ante, p. 24-25. † Ante, p. 26. ‡ Mysore Papers, p. 90.

nounced that the Nawab had been "established by the East India Company in the rank, property and possessions of his ancestors, heretofore Nabobs of the Carnatic."

Lord Wellesley attached so little importance to the alteration, that he expressly cautioned Lord Clive that it should not be proposed to Azeem-ood-Dowlah "*at the hazard of exciting any alarm or jealousy in his Highness's mind,*" or of incurring his "*dissent or displeasure.*"* And in the mean time, anticipating the possibility of Azeem-ood-Dowlah's objections, Lord Wellesley ratified the original Treaty. But the modified Preamble was accepted by the Nawab without discussion.

There was no necessity for inserting the words "heirs and successors" in the Carnatic Treaty of 1801, because its second Article expressly "renewed and confirmed" all the former Treaties, which contained ample guaranties of hereditary succession. And the alteration suggested and carried out by Lord Wellesley was not aimed at hereditary succession, but against the inherent and independent right and power of the Nawab to succeed to the throne, at a political crisis, without British sanction and support. I am fully convinced that Lord Wellesley had no more notion of making a personal Treaty with the Nawab of Arcot than with the Rajah of Mysore. But having pointed out that Mr. Prinsep's citation of the Carnatic case is completely erroneous and unfounded, consisting in fact of a misquotation, I am relieved from any call to notice it further.

I may mention, however, that Mr. Mangles also refers to the Carnatic case as "a precedent."† I can only say that it is fully as worthy of being a precedent as the case of Sattara.

Before finally concluding my task I must ask Mr. Mangles whether he can, on serious reflection, reconcile it with his notions of public duty to have failed so flagrantly in accuracy and precision of statement and reference, throughout his Minute of Consultation, as I have proved him to have done. He was selected for the honourable position of a

* Carnatic Papers, 1861, p. 109, 110.

† Mysore Papers, p. 84 (*note*). I have discussed the Carnatic case in *The Empire in India.*

Councillor to her Majesty's Government in a special department, from trust in his professional experience, and his long familiarity with bygone transactions recorded in the voluminous chronicles of the India Office, with which no Secretary of State can become immediately conversant. If the Minister can place no reliance on statements of fact and quotations of public documents laid before him by his confidential advisers, the Council will be a snare to him rather than an assistance. He had much better trust to humbler aid. No clerk, no *précis* writer, no Under Secretary would venture to mislead the head of his Office as Mr. Mangles has done, and would certainly not be allowed to do so twice. For the worst derelictions with which I have charged Mr. Mangles are not to be palliated by a plea of carelessness or inadvertence. The best sources of information, the best means of verification lay within his reach, and the specific assertions of which I complain, can be found nowhere at the India Office, except in his own Minute.

And in my humble opinion it is just because Mr. Mangles is not open to reproof and correction as a subordinate official, but is invested with the sacred and judicial character of a Councillor, and associated as a colleague with the Secretary of State, that he should be held to a stricter account by the Government and by the country. Although not a subordinate official, he is now a salaried public servant. In his former capacity as a Director of the East India Company, he was not exactly a servant of the public, owing merely a nominal responsibility to his constituents in the Court of Proprietors. And in the House of Commons, a few occasional loose and rash assertions and contradictions may be excused, in a man of a certain temperament, from considerations of the heat of debate, the urgency of immediate reply, and the absence of the records required. If Mr. Mangles, as Member for Guildford, had assured the House of Commons that "Mysore was now full of European settlers, and that every day was adding to their numbers," the enormity even of this exaggeration might have been passed over or pardoned, as a sudden flight of rhetoric called forth in the excitement of a party struggle, or in defending the credit of the Court of Directors.

But what might be tolerated and forgiven in a speech, is quite inadmissible and inexcusable in a consultative Minute, penned in cold blood, in the calm retirement of a room at the India Office, with access to every piece of information connected with the subject, and every opinion that has ever been passed upon it.

Notwithstanding the good intentions for which Mr. Mangles may receive full credit, it must not be forgotten that he is committed beyond retreat to a policy of unrelenting annexation, by his active participation in all the territorial acquisitions of the last twenty years, from Sattara to Oude. He could not spare Mysore without condemning all his previous utterances and exertions. In truth Mr. Mangles has always manifested, and manifests most signally in this particular case, that unjudicial frame of mind which seems the peculiar growth of those Calcutta bureaux to which his Indian experience was confined. From extensive research among the Minutes and Despatches of Indian Governors and Councillors in the leading political cases of the last twenty years, I have been struck with the general prevalence of the same unjudicial method. Instead of starting with a straightforward determination to settle the points of right and wrong, with few exceptions each Councillor has evidently begun by deciding what arrangement will be the most advantageous for all parties, with especial regard to the supposed interests of his own Government, and has then set to work to concoct ingenious and elaborate pretexts for carrying out the desired arrangement. There is no actual insincerity, no disingenuous perversion of the truth, but an unmistakeable subordination of judgment, logic and law to the political and social results that are expected and desired, and a dexterous adaptation of the premisses to meet the required conclusion. And when I see unmistakeable evidence both of national prejudice and professional bias, I neither question nor value benevolent motives.

I have pointed out some errors of fact into which Mr. Prinsep has fallen. Himself an old Bengal Civilian, he betrays in his Minute the characteristic want of personal and class sympathy for those who are to be despoiled and degraded, and an utter contempt for the feelings and wishes of the people of Mysore. And moreover it would hardly be consistent with human nature if Mr. Prinsep were entirely free from a very strong though probably unconscious bias against the Rajah. Mr. H. T. Prinsep, as Foreign Secretary, signed all the despatches in 1831, by which the suspension of his Highness's authority was explained and carried out. Even the severe letter from Lord William Bentinck to the Rajah, of September 7th, 1831, announcing that he was about to assume the management of Mysore,—that letter which contains at least two erroneous charges against the Rajah, first, that "*the Subsidy had not been paid monthly according to the Treaty,*"* and second, that "*the greatest excesses were committed and unparalleled cruelties inflicted by his Highness's officers,*"†—was issued from his office, and according to the ordinary routine must have been drafted by himself. Of course these charges were brought against the Rajah, probably in stronger terms, in all the despatches home. In his Minute of the 1st August 1865, Mr. Prinsep does not repeat these accusations, but he does not withdraw them. When the Report of the Special Commissioners of Inquiry, dated the 12th December, 1833, which dispelled several of the imputations cast upon the Rajah's rule and personal conduct, and opened Lord William Bentinck's eyes to the wrong that had been committed, was submitted to the Government of India, Mr. Prinsep was no longer Foreign Secretary, but had been replaced by Mr. (afterwards Sir W. H.) Macnaghten, who was always favourable to the Rajah's reinstatement.

In conclusion I would say, if the Rajah is ever to be reinstated, it should not done as a half-measure, but with a definite purpose and policy. The object should not be that of pleasing, consoling, and flattering an aged Prince, and smoothing the transition of Mysore into an ordinary British Province. The ultimate object, even though postponed till the young Prince's majority, should be that of preserving the Principality, and maintaining the Treaties of 1799 inviolate. No measure of compensation and com-

* The Subsidy was proved not only never to have been a month in arrears, but to have been paid in advance (Mysore Papers, p. 64).

† Ante, p. 7; and *Mysore Reversion*, 2nd edition, p. 25, 27. The letter will be found entire in Appendix C to the *Mysore Reversion*.

promise, however liberal, will save the honour of Great Britain, relieve the alarmed and outraged feelings of the Princes of India, or secure to the Imperial Power the full advantages of a reformed Native State. We do not want the Rajah of Mysore as a pageant, or as a nobleman, or as a pensioner, but as a tributary and protected Sovereign, ruling his own territories according to our views and principles, acting for us as a Conservative agent, as the symbol of law and allegiance.

The policy and practice of the rulers of India have been necessarily modified by circumstances. The experiment even of unrelenting appropriations was perhaps inevitable for a time; nor do I think it was carried too far, until we began absorbing friendly and faithful dependencies,—until, as Sir George Clerk says, "the Calcutta Government led off with the bare-faced appropriation of Sattara".* We need not condemn or deplore the exploits of our predecessors. It was necessary to restore order; it was necessary to produce submission. The rule, the very idea of law—unmixed with religious and ceremonial sanctions and exemptions,—was introduced, and could only have been established by the hands of our countrymen. But the perpetual degradation of our docile pupils cannot be essential to British supremacy. Slavery, or polygamy, or the feudal system may have been necessary to human progress in a certain age and region, and may therefore have been justifiable; but it does not follow that these historical conditions are either necessary or justifiable now.

We want the Native Princes of India much more than they want us. We cannot get near the people without the good will of their natural leaders. We want them both for the discipline and the education of that vast population. Mr. Gladstone eloquently observed in his speech of the 12th March last:—"When we are told that affairs are managed more economically, more cleverly, and effectually in foreign countries, we answer, 'Yes, but here they are managed freely; and in freedom, in the free discharge of political duties, there is an immense power both of discipline and of education for the people'." The nearest approach to political freedom that the people of India can make in their present

* Mysore Papers, p. 72.

phase of civilisation, must be made by means of reformed Native States, owning allegiance and subordination to the Imperial Power. The British Government of India should not attempt to be ubiquitously executive ; it should be constructive and critical, not operative ; it should everywhere contrive and control the organisation, but wherever native agency is available, it should not undertake more than the superintendence of functions.

Even if natives administer judicial and financial affairs worse than English officers,—which I do not admit,—Native Princes, when once put in the right way, can govern much more effectually and economically for themselves as well as for us, than English Commissioners. And even if we are not at present prepared to increase the number or the area of our reformed Native dependencies, let us not, at an immense sacrifice of honour and moral influence, strike out of our system the most prosperous and to us the most profitable of them all, by reverting to an abandoned policy, and reasserting a usurped and disclaimed prerogative.

APPENDIX.

PARTITION TREATY OF MYSORE, 1799.

*Treaty for strengthening the Alliance and Friendship subsisting between the English East-India Company Behauder, his Highness the Nabob Nizam-ul-Dowlah Asoph Jah Behauder, and the Paishwah, Row Pundit Purdhaun Behauder, and for effecting a Settlement of the Dominions of the late Tippoo Sultaun.**

Whereas the deceased Tippoo Sultaun, unprovoked by any act of aggression on the part of the Allies, entered into an offensive and defensive alliance with the French, and admitted a French force into his army, for the purpose of commencing war against the Honourable English Company Behauder, and its Allies, Nizam-ul-Dowlah Asoph Jah Behauder, and the Paishwah Row Pundit Purdhaun Behauder; and the said Tippoo Sultaun having attempted to evade the just demands of satisfaction and security made by the Honourable English Company and its Allies, for their defence and protection against the joint designs of the said Sultaun and of the French, the allied armies of the Honourable English Company Behauder and of his Highness Nizam-ul-Dowlah Asoph Jah Behauder proceeded to hostilities, in vindication of their rights, and for the preservation of their respective dominions from the perils of foreign invasion, and from the ravages of a cruel and relentless enemy.

And whereas it has pleased Almighty God to prosper the just cause of the said Allies, the Honourable English Company Behauder and his Highness Nizam-ul-Dowlah Asoph Jah Behauder, with a continual course of victory and success, and finally to crown their arms by the reduction of the capital of Mysore, the fall of Tippoo Sultaun, the utter extinction of his power, and the unconditional submission of his people; and whereas the said Allies, being disposed to exercise the rights of conquest with the same moderation and forbearance which they have observed from the commencement to the conclusion of the late successful war, have resolved to use the power which it has pleased Almighty God to place in their hands, for the purpose of obtaining reasonable compensation for the expenses of the war, and of establishing permanent security and genuine tranquillity for themselves and their subjects, as well as for all the powers contiguous to their respective dominions; wherefore a Treaty, for the adjustment of the territories of the late Tippoo Sultaun between the English East-India Company Behauder and his

* The Paishwah refused to accede to this Treaty.

Highness the Nabob Nizam-ul-Dowlah Asoph Jah Behauder, is now concluded by Lieutenant General George Harris, Commander in Chief of the Forces of his Britannic Majesty and of the English East-India Company Behauder in the Carnatic and on the Coast of Malabar, the Honourable Colonel Arthur Wellesley, the Honourable Henry Wellesley, Lieutenant Colonel William Kirkpatrick, and Lieutenant Colonel Barry Close, on the part and in the name of the Right Honourable Richard Earl of Mornington, K.P., Governor General for all Affairs, civil and military, of the British Nation in India; and by the Nabob Meer Allum Behauder, on the part and in the name of his Highness the Nabob Nizam-ul-Dowlah Asoph Jah Behauder, according to the under-mentioned Articles, which, by the blessing of God, shall be binding upon the heirs and successors of the contracting parties, as long as the sun and moon shall endure, and of which the conditions shall be reciprocally observed by the said contracting parties.

I. It being reasonable and just, that the Allies by this Treaty should accomplish the original objects of the war (*viz.* a due indemnification for the expenses incurred in their own defence, and effectual security for their respective possessions against the future designs of their enemies), it is stipulated and agreed, that the districts specified in the Schedule A, hereunto annexed, together with the heads of all the passes leading from the territory of the late Tippoo Sultaun to any part of the possessions of the English East-India Company Behauder, of its Allies or tributaries, situated between the Ghauts on either coast, and all forts situated near to and commanding the said passes, shall be subjected to the authority, and be for ever incorporated with the dominions of the English East-India Company Behauder, the said Company Behauder engaging to provide effectually out of the revenues of the said districts, for the suitable maintenance of the whole of the families of the late Hyder Ali Khan and of the late Tippoo Sultaun, and to apply to this purpose, with the reservation hereinafter stated, an annual sum of not less than two lacs of Star Pagodas, making the Company's share as follows:

Estimated value of districts enumerated in the Schedule A, according to the statement of Tippoo Sultaun in 1792 - - - - Canterai Pagodas	7,77,170
Deduct, provision for the families of Hyder Ali Khan and of Tippoo Sultaun, two lacs of Star Pagodas, in Canterai Pagodas - - - - - -	2,40,000
Remains to the East India Company - - - -	5,37,170

II. For the same reason stated in the preceding Articles, the district specified in Schedule B, annexed hereunto, shall be subjected to the authority, and for ever united to the dominions of the Nabob Nizam-ul-Dowlah Asoph Jah Behauder, the said Nabob having engaged to provide liberally, from the revenues of the said districts, for the support of Meer Kummer-ud-Dien Khan Behauder, and of his family and relations, and to grant him for this purpose a personal Jaghire in the districts of Gurrumcondah equal to the annual sum of 2,10,000 rupees, or of 70,000 Canterai Pagodas, over and above and exclusive of a Jaghire, which the said Nabob has also agreed to assign to the said Meer Kummer-ud-Dien Khan, for the pay and maintenance of a proportionate number of troops to be employed in the service of his said Highness, making the share of his Highness as follows:

Estimated value of the territory specified in Schedule B, according to the statement of Tippoo Sultaun in 1792 - - - Canterai Pagodas	6,07,332
Deduct, personal Jaghire to Meer Kummer-ud-Dien Khan, 2,10,000 rupees, or - - - - -	70,000
Remains to the Nabob Nizam-ud-Dowlah Asoph Jah Behauder - - - - - - - - -	5,37,332

III. It being farther expedient for the preservation of peace and tranquillity, and for the general security, on the foundations now established by the contracting parties, that the fortress of Seringapatam should be subjected to the said Company Behauder, it is stipulated and agreed that the said fortress, and the island on which it is situated (including the small tract of land, or island, lying to the westward of the main island, and bounded on the west by a Nullah, called the Mysore Nullah, which falls into the Cauvery near Chenagal Ghaut) shall become part of the dominions of the said Company, in full right and sovereignty for ever.

IV. A separate Government shall be established in Mysore; and for this purpose, it is stipulated and agreed, that the Maha Rajah Mysore Kishna Rajah Oodiaver Behauder, a descendant of the ancient Rajahs of Mysore, shall possess the territory hereinafter described, upon the conditions hereinafter mentioned.

V. The contracting powers mutually and severally agree, that the districts specified in Schedule C, hereunto annexed, shall be ceded to the said Maha Rajah Mysore Kishna Rajah, and shall form the separate Government of Mysore, upon the conditions hereinafter mentioned.

VI. The English East India Company Behauder shall be at liberty to make such deductions, from time to time, from the sums allotted by the first Article of the present Treaty, for the maintenance of the families of Hyder Ali Khan and Tippoo Sultaun, as may be proper, in consequence of the decease of any member of the said families; and in the event of any hostile attempt, on the part of the said family, or of any member of it, against the authority of the contracting parties, or against the peace of their respective dominions, or the territories of the Rajah of Mysore, then the said English East India Company Behauder shall be at liberty to limit or suspend entirely the payment of the whole, or any part of the stipend hereinbefore stipulated to be applied to the maintenance and support of the said families.

VII. His Highness the Paishwa Row Pundit Purdhaun Behauder shall be invited to accede to the present Treaty; and although the said Paishwah Row Pundit Purdhaun Behauder has neither participated in the expense or danger of the late war, and therefore is not entitled to share any part of the acquisitions made by the contracting parties (namely, the English East India Company Behauder and his Highness the Nabob Nizam-ud-Dowlah Asoph Jah Behauder), yet for the maintenance of the relations of friendship and alliance between the said Paishwa Row Pundit Purdhaun Behauder, the English East India Company Behauder, his Highness the Nabob Nizam-ud-Dowlah Asoph Jah Behauder, and Maha Rajah Mysore Kishna Rajah Behauder, it is stipulated and agreed that certain districts, specified in Schedule D, hereunto annexed, shall be reserved for the purpose of being eventually ceded to the said Paishwah Row Pundit Purdhaun Behauder, in full right and sovereignty, in the same manner as if he had been a contracting party to this Treaty; provided, however, that the said Paishwa Row Pundit Purdhaun Behauder shall accede to the present Treaty, in its full extent, within one month from the day on which it shall be formally communicated to him by the contracting parties, and provided also that he shall give satisfaction to the English East India Company Behauder, and to his Highness Nizam-ud-Dowlah Asoph Jah Behauder, with regard to certain points now depending between him, the said Paishwa Row Pundit Purdhaun Behauder, and the said Nabob Nizam-ud-Dowlah Asoph Jah Behauder, and also with regard to such points as shall be represented to the said Paishwah, on the part of the English East India Company Behauder, by the Governor General or the British Resident at the Court of Poonah.

VIII. If, contrary to the amicable expectation of the contracting parties, the said Paishwah Row Pundit Purdhaun Behauder shall refuse to accede to this Treaty, or to give satisfaction upon the points to which the Seventh Article refers, then the right to, and sovereignty of, the several districts hereinbefore reserved for eventual cession to the Paishwah Row Pundit Purdhaun Behauder, shall rest jointly in the said English East India Company Behauder and the said Nabob Nizam-ud-Dowlah Asoph Jah Behauder, who will either exchange them with the Rajah of Mysore for other districts of equal value, more contiguous to their respective territories, or otherwise arrange and settle respecting them, as they shall judge proper.

IX. It being expedient for the effectual establishment of Maha Rajah Mysore Kishna Rajah in the Government of Mysore, that his Highness should be assisted with a suitable Subsidiary Force, it is stipulated and agreed, that the whole of the said Force shall be furnished by the English East India Company Behauder, according to the terms of a separate Treaty, to be immediately concluded between the said English East India Company Behauder and his Highness the Maha Rajah Mysore Kishna Rajah Oodiaver Behauder.

X. This Treaty, consisting of ten Articles, being settled and concluded this day, the 22d of June, 1799 (corresponding to the 17th of Mohurrun, 1214 Anno Hegiræ) by Lieutenant General George Harris, the Honourable Colonel Arthur Wellesley, the Honourable Henry Wellesley, Lieutenant Colonel William Kirkpatrick, and Lieutenant Colonel Barry Close, on the part and in the name of the Right Honourable Richard Earl of Mornington, Governor General aforesaid; and by Meer Allum Behauder on the part and in the name of His Highness the Nabob Nizam-ud-Dowlah Asoph Jah Behauder; the said Lieutenant General Harris, the Honourable Colonel Arthur Wellesley, the Honourable Henry Wellesley, Lieutenant Colonel William Kirkpatrick, and Lieutenant Colonel Barry Close, have delivered to Meer Allum Behauder one copy of the same, signed and sealed by themselves; and Meer Allum Behauder has delivered to Lieutenant General George Harris, the Honourable Colonel Arthur Wellesley, the Honourable Henry Wellesley, Lieutenant Colonel William Kirkpatrick, and Lieutenant Colonel Barry Close, another copy of the same, sealed by himself; and Lieutenant General George Harris, the Honourable Colonel Arthur Wellesley, the Honourable Henry Wellesley, Lieutenant Colonel William Kirkpatrick, and Lieutenant Colonel Barry Close, and Meer Allum Behauder, severally and mutually engage, that the said Treaty shall be respectively ratified by the Right Honourable the Governor General, under his seal and signature, within eight days from the date hereof, and by his Highness the Nabob Nizam-ud-Dowlah Asoph Jah Behauder, within twenty-five days from the date hereof. Ratified at Hyderabad, by his Highness the Nizam, on the 13th day of July, Anno Domini 1799.

(Signed) J. A. KIRKPATRICK, *Resident.*

Schedule A (*The Company's Share*).

* * * *

Schedule B (*The Nizam's Share*).

* * * *

Schedule C (*Districts ceded to Maha Rajah Mysore Kishna Rajah Oodiaver Behauder.*)

* * * *

SEPARATE ARTICLES OF THE TREATY WITH THE NIZAM.

Separate Articles appertaining to the Treaty of Mysore, concluded on the 22nd of June, 1799 (corresponding to the 17th of Mohurrum, Anno Hegiræ 1214) between the Honourable English East India Company Behauder, and the Nabob Nizam-ul-Dowlah Asoph Jah Behauder.

I. With a view to the prevention of future altercations, it is agreed between his Highness the Nabob Nizam-ud-Dowlah Asoph Jah Behauder and the Honourable English East India Company Behauder, that to whatever amount the stipends appropriated to the maintenance of the sons, relations, and dependants of the late Hyder Ali Khan and Tippoo Sultaun, or the personal Jaghire of Meer Kummer-ud-Deen Khan, shall hereafter be diminished, in consequence of any one of the stipulations of the Treaty of Mysore, the contracting parties shall not be accountable to each other on this head.

II. And it is further agreed between the contracting parties, that in the event provided for by the Eighth Article of the Treaty of Mysore, two-thirds of the share reserved for Row Pundit Purdhaun Behauder shall fall to his Highness the Nabob Nizam-ud-Dowlah Asoph Jah Behauder, and the remaining third to the Honourable English East India Company Behauder.

Ratified at Hyderabad by his Highness the Nizam,
on the 13th day of July, Anno Domini 1799.

(*Signed*) J. A. KIRKPATRICK, *Resident.*

SUBSIDIARY TREATY OF SERINGAPATAM, 1799.

A Treaty of perpetual Friendship and Alliance, concluded on the one part by his Excellency Lieutenant-General George Harris, Commander in Chief of the Forces of his Britannic Majesty and of the English East India Company Behauder in the Carnatic and on the Coast of Malabar, the Honourable Colonel Arthur Wellesley, the Honourable Henry Wellesley, Lieutenant Colonel William Kirkpatrick, and Lieutenant-Colonel Barry Close, on behalf and in the name of the Right Honourable Richard Earl of Mornington, K.P., Governor General for all Affairs, civil and military, of the British Nation in India, by virtue of full powers vested in them for this purpose by the said Richard Earl of Mornington, Governor General; and on the other part by Maha Rajah Mysore Kistna Rajah Oodiaver Behauder, Rajah of Mysore.

Whereas it is stipulated, in the Treaty concluded on the 22nd of June, 1799, between the Honourable English East India Company Behauder, and the Nabob Nizam-ud-Dowlah Asoph

Jah Behauder, for strengthening the alliance and friendship subsisting between the said English East India Company Behauder, his Highness Nizam-ud-Dowlah Asoph Jah Behauder, and the Peshwa, Row Pundit Purdhaun Behauder, and for effecting a settlement of the territories of the late Tippoo Sultaun, that a separate Government shall be established in Mysore, and that his Highness Maha Rajah Mysore Kistna Rajah Oodiaver Behauder shall possess certain territories, specified in Schedule C, annexed to the said Treaty, and that, for the effectual establishment of the Government of Mysore, his Highness shall be assisted with a suitable Subsidiary Force, to be furnished by the English East India Company Behauder; wherefore, in order to carry the said stipulations into effect, and to increase and strengthen the friendship subsisting between the said English East India Company and the said Maha Rajah Mysore Kistna Rajah Oodiaver Behauder, this Treaty is concluded by Lieutenant-General George Harris, Commander in Chief of the Forces of his Britannic Majesty and of the said English East India Company Behauder in the Carnatic and on the Coast of Malabar, the Honourable Colonel Arthur Wellesley, the Honourable Henry Wellesley, Lieutenant Colonel William Kirkpatrick, and Lieutenant Colonel Barry Close, on the part and in the name of the Right Honourable Richard Earl of Mornington, Governor General aforesaid, and by his Highness Maha Rajah Mysore Kishna Rajah Oodiaver Behauder, which shall be binding upon the contracting parties as long as the sun and moon shall endure.

I. The friends and enemies of either of the contracting parties shall be considered as the friends and enemies of both.

II. The Honourable East India Company Behauder agrees to maintain, and his Highness Maha Rajah Mysore Kistna Rajah Oodiaver Behauder agrees to receive, a military force, for the defence and security of his Highness's dominions; in consideration of which protection, his Highness engages to pay the annual sum of seven lacks of Star Pagodas to the said East-India Company, the said sum to be paid in twelve equal monthly instalments, commencing from the 1st of July, Anno Domini 1799. And his Highness further agrees, that the disposal of the said sum, together with the arrangement and employment of the troops to be maintained by it, shall be entirely left to the Company.

III. If it shall be necessary for the protection and defence of the territories of the contracting parties, or of either of them, that hostilities shall be undertaken, or preparations made for commencing hostilities against any State or Power, his said Highness Maha Rajah Mysore Kistna Rajah Oodiaver Behauder, agrees to contribute towards the discharge of the increased expense incurred by the augmentation of the military force, and the unavoidable charges of war, such a sum as shall appear to the

Governor General in Council of Fort William, on an attentive consideration of the means of his said Highness, to bear a just and reasonable proportion to the actual net revenues of his said Highness.

IV. And whereas it is indispensably necessary, that effectual and lasting security should be provided against any failure in the funds destined to defray either the expenses of the permanent military force in time of peace, or the extraordinary expenses described in the Third Article of the present Treaty, it is hereby stipulated and agreed between the contracting parties, that whenever the Governor General in Council of Fort William in Bengal shall have reason to apprehend such failure in the funds so destined, the said Governor General in Council shall be at liberty, and shall have full power and right, either to introduce such regulations and ordinances as he shall deem expedient for the internal management and collection of the revenues, or for the better ordering of any other branch and department of the Government of Mysore, or to assume and bring under the direct management of the servants of the said Company Behauder, such part or parts of the territorial possessions of his Highness Maha Rajah Mysore Kistna Rajah Oodiaver Behauder, as shall appear to him, the said Governor General in Council, necessary to render the said funds efficient and available either in time of peace or war.

V. And it is hereby further agreed, that whenever the said Governor General in Council shall signify to the said Maha Rajah Mysore Kistna Rajah Oodiaver Behauder, that it is become necessary to carry into effect the provisions of the Fourth Article, his said Highness Maha Rajah Mysore Kistna Rajah Oodiaver Behauder shall immediately issue orders to his Aumils, or other officers, either for carrying into effect the said regulations and ordinances, according to the tenor of the Fourth Article, or for placing the territories required under the exclusive authority and control of the English Company Behauder. And in case his Highness shall not issue such orders within ten days from the time when the application shall have been formally made to him, then the said Governor General in Council shall be at liberty to issue orders, by his own authority, either for carrying into effect the regulations and ordinances, or for assuming the management and collection of the revenue of the said territories, as he shall judge most expedient for the purpose of securing the efficiency of the said military funds, and of providing for the effectual protection of the country and the welfare of the people. Provided always, that whenever, and so long as any part or parts of his said Highness's territories shall be placed, and shall remain under the exclusive authority and control of the said East India Company, the Governor General in Council shall render to his Highness a true and faithful account of the revenues and produce of the territories so assumed; provided also, that in no case whatever shall his Highness's actual receipts or actual income, arising out of his territorial revenue, be less than the sum of one lac of Star Pagodas, together with one-fifth of the net revenue of the whole of the territories ceded to him by the Fifth Article of the Treaty of Mysore; which sum of one lac of Star Pagodas, together with the amount of one-fifth of the said net revenue, the East India Company engages, at all times and in every possible case, to secure and cause to be paid for his Highness's use.

VI. His Highness Maha Rajah Mysore Kistna Rajah Oodiaver Behauder engages, that he will be guided by a sincere and cordial attention to the relations of peace and amity, now established between the English Company Behauder and their Allies, and that he will carefully abstain from any interference in the affairs of any State in alliance with the said English Company Behauder, or of any State whatever. And for securing the object of this stipulation, it is further stipulated and agreed, that no communication or correspondence with any foreign State whatever, shall be holden by his said Highness without the previous knowledge and sanction of the said English Company Behauder.

VII. His Highness stipulates and agrees, that he will not admit any European foreigners into his service, without the concurrence of the English Company Behauder; and that he will apprehend and deliver up to the Company's Government all Europeans, of whatever description, who shall be found within the territories of his said Highness, without regular passports from the Company's Government, it being his Highness's determined resolution not to suffer, even for a day, any European foreigners to remain within the territories now subjected to his authority, unless by consent of the said Company.

VIII. Whereas the complete protection of his Highness's said territories requires that various fortresses and strong places, situated within the territories of his Highness, should be garrisoned and commanded, as well in time of peace as of war, by British troops and officers, his Highness Maha Rajah Mysore Kistna Rajah Oodiaver Behauder engages, that the said English Company Behauder shall at all times be at liberty to garrison, in whatever manner they may judge proper, all such fortresses and strong places, within his said Highness's territories, as it shall appear advisable to them to take charge of.

IX. And whereas, in consequence of the system of defence which it may be expedient to adopt, for the security of the territorial possessions of his Highness Maha Rajah Mysoor Kistna Rajah Oodiaver Behauder, it may be necessary that certain forts and strong places, within his Highness's territories, should be dismantled or destroyed, and that other forts and strong places should be strengthened and repaired, it is stipulated and agreed, that the English East-India Company Behauder shall be the sole judges of the necessity of any such alterations in the said fortresses; and it is further agreed, that such expences as may be incurred on this account, shall be borne and defrayed, in equal proportions, by the contracting parties.

X. In case it shall become necessary, for enforcing and maintaining the authority and government of his Highness in the territories now subjected to his power, that the regular troops of the English East-India Company Behauder should be employed, it is stipulated and agreed, that upon formal application being made for the service of the said troops, they shall be employed in such manner as to the said Company shall seem fit: but it is expressly understood by the contracting parties, that this stipulation shall not subject the troops of the English East-India Company Behauder to be employed in the ordinary transactions of revenue.

XI. It being expedient for the restoration and permanent establishment of tranquillity in the territories now subjected to the authority of his Highness Maha Rajah Mysoor Kistna Rajah Oodiaver Behauder, that suitable provision should be made for certain officers of rank in the service of the late Tippoo Sultaun, his said Highness agrees to enter into the immediate discussion of this point, and to fix the amount of the funds (as soon as the necessary information can be obtained) to be granted for this purpose, in a separate Article, to be hereafter added to this Treaty.

XII. Lest the garrison of Seringapatam should, at any time, be subject to inconvenience from the high price of provisions and other necessaries, his Highness Maha Rajah Mysore Kistna Rajah Oodiaver Behauder agrees, that such quantities of provisions and other necessaries, as may be required for the use and consumption of the troops composing the said garrison, shall be allowed to enter the place, from all and every part of his dominions, free of any duty, tax, or impediment whatever.

XIII. The contracting parties hereby agree to take into their early consideration the best means of establishing such a commercial intercourse between their respective dominions, as shall be mutually beneficial to the subjects of both Governments, and to conclude a Commercial Treaty for this purpose, with as little delay as possible.

XIV. His Highness Maha Rajah Mysore Kistna Rajah Oodiaver Behauder hereby promises to pay at all times the utmost attention to such advice as the Company's Government shall occasionally judge it necessary to offer to him, with a view to the economy of his finances, the better collection of his revenues, the administration of justice, the extension of commerce, the encouragement of trade, agriculture, and industry, or any other objects connected with the advancement of his Highness's interests, the happiness of his people, and the mutual welfare of both States.

XV. Whereas it may hereafter appear, that some of the districts declared by the Treaty of Mysore to belong respectively to the English Company Behauder and to his Highness are inconveniently situated, with a view to the proper connection of their respective lines of frontier, it is hereby stipulated between the contracting parties, that in all such cases they will proceed to such an adjustment, by means of exchanges or otherwise, as shall be best suited to the occasion.

XVI. This Treaty, consisting of sixteen Articles, being this day, the 8th of July, Anno Domini 1799 (corresponding to the 3rd of Suffur, Anno Hegiræ 1214, and to the 7th of the month Assar, of 1721st year of the Saliwahan era) settled and concluded at the fort of Nazzerbagh, near Seringapatam, by his Excellency, Lieutenant-General George Harris, Commander-in-Chief of the Forces of his Britannic Majesty, and of the Honourable English East India Company Behauder, in the Carnatic and on the Coast of Malabar, the Honourable Colonel Arthur Wellesley, the Honourable Henry Wellesley, Lieutenant-Colonel William Kirkpatrick, and Lieutenant-Colonel Barry Close, with the Maha Rajah Mysore Kistna Rajah Oodiaver Behauder, the aforesaid gentlemen have delivered to the said Maha Rajah one copy of the same, in English and Persian, sealed and signed by them, and his Highness the Maha Rajah has delivered to the gentlemen aforesaid another copy, also in Persian and English, bearing his seal, and signed by Luchuma, widow of the late Kistna Rajah, and sealed and signed by Purnia, Dewan to the Maha Rajah Kistna Rajah Oodiaver. And the aforesaid gentlemen have engaged to procure and to deliver to the said Maha Rajah, without delay, a copy of the same, under the seal and signature of the Right Honourable the Governor General, on the receipt of which by the said Maha Rajah, the present Treaty shall be demed complete and binding on the Honourable the English East India Company and on the Maha Rajah Mysore Kistna Rajah Oodiaver Behauder, and the copy of it now delivered to the said Maha Rajah shall be returned.

Witnessed *(Seal of the Maha Rajah)*

(Signed) EDWARD GOLDING, and the

Assistant Secretary. *(Ranee's Signature.)*

(Seal and Signature of Purniah.)

A true Copy,

(Signed) G. BUCHAN,

Sub-Secretary.